STOLEN CHILDHOOD

STOLEN CHILDHOOD

TESTIMONIES OF THE SURVIVORS OF CHILD SEXUAL ABUSE

ISEULT O'DOHERTY

POOLBEG

Published 1998
by Poolbeg Press Ltd
123 Baldoyle Industrial Estate
Dublin 13, Ireland

© Iseult O'Doherty 1998

The moral right of the author has been asserted.

A catalogue record for this book is available from the British Library.

ISBN 1 85371 708 8

All rights reserved. No part of this publication may be reproduced or transmitted in any form or by any means, electronic or mechanical, including photography, recording, or any information storage or retrieval system, without permission in writing from the publisher. The book is sold subject to the condition that it shall not, by way of trade or otherwise, be lent, resold or otherwise circulated without the publisher's prior consent in any form of binding or cover other than that in which it is published and without a similar condition, including this condition, being imposed on the subsequent purchaser.

Cover design by Poolbeg Group Services Ltd
Set by Poolbeg Group Services Ltd in Stone 10/14
Printed by The Guernsey Press Ltd,
Vale, Guernsey, Channel Islands.

ACKNOWLEDGEMENTS

My deepest thanks go to all those people who shared the most intimate and painful details of their lives with me. For their trust and courage I will be always grateful. A special thanks to those whose stories are told in this book. They agreed to do so in the hope that they might help others.

Thanks also to all of my colleagues in the *Would You Believe* programme, especially researcher, Brenda Moran, who handled so many phone calls and producer, Con Bushe, for his patience and support. To the rest of the team who weathered the storm – Kevin Dawson, Gemma McCrohan, Anne McLoughlin, Mick Peelo, Anna C Ryan and Jim Skelly – thanks for everything.

Thanks to Kate Cruise O'Brien for having faith in this idea and for her sensitivity and insight. A big thanks to Mary Maher, who had the unenviable task of editing this book, for her patience and good sense.

Finally, thanks to all my family and friends for their constant support during the tough times. But most of all thanks to Myles and our children Amber, Rory, Lara and Ross who put up with me hunched over a computer for endless hours – when I could have been having fun with them.

The names, locations and physical descriptions of some of the people who appear in this book have been changed to protect their identities.

To all my family with all my love.

CONTENTS

CHAPTER ONE	1
GERALDINE	11
PAT	43
MOLLY	73
DEREK	103
ANNE	135
MICHAELA	169
HELPFUL NUMBERS	195
SOME HELP NUMBER IN THE UK	206
USEFUL BOOKS	207

CHAPTER ONE

A few years ago the first reports of child sexual abuse started to appear in the papers. Slowly the number of reports grew until it seemed as if every day a new, and often more terrible, story surfaced. There were bald accounts of trials with brief descriptions of the events that had taken place, cold legal terminology describing human acts of real depravity. Defendants were seldom named in order to protect the identity of their victims. The victims of these crimes had to face questioning from barristers designed to elicit every detail of their abuse. Their abusers sat in the same room.

Those who were able to face all of this, added to their own shame and pain, sometimes saw their abusers found guilty. Sentences were handed down and justice, of a sort, was seen to be done.

But what happened to these abused people afterwards? Where did they go? How did they live? Were their lives shattered beyond redemption? These nameless people, unnamed to protect their identities felt as if they had done something wrong. The shame was seen to be theirs.

Slowly the idea grew in my mind that these people might have something to say. In a country that still prides itself on its humanity and Christianity it would be interesting to see how some of them had fared. Maybe they would be willing to tell their story on television. I was working on a weekly religious documentary series in RTE and the idea was put to the programme team. It was accepted enthusiastically (little did we realise the storm we were about to unleash on ourselves). The programme, *Would You Believe*, covers a vast array of topics including issues of justice, morality, social equality and religious beliefs. The effects of abuse on people's spirituality and self-esteem fell well within the remit of our programme.

The next task was to find people who were willing to talk about a subject that had been taboo in Ireland for generations. Following the suggestion of a colleague I wrote a letter to the national newspapers asking people who had experienced abuse to contact the programme. *The Irish Times* published the letter one Saturday in February 1996.

The following Monday morning I went into work and the phones started ringing. They rang all day, every day, for over two weeks. Tales of abuse and all its horror and misery poured down the phone lines. Everybody in the office was answering phones, taking down numbers and promising that I or my researcher colleague, Brenda Moran, would ring back.

Towards the end of that first day I phoned *The Irish Independent* and *The Irish Press* (still in operation at the time) and asked them not to publish the letter I had sent them. We simply could not cope with the volume of calls we were receiving.

Throughout the night messages were left on our answering machines by those who had been unable, or unwilling, to get through during the day. For more than two weeks Brenda and I returned people's calls and listened to their stories. I went home every night with a list of names and numbers to phone back. Each evening I spent hours on the phone listening to people crying of their pain. There was so much of it. I began to see abuse everywhere. Was there anybody who had not been abused?

For many people it was the first time they had spoken of their abuse. For some reason they seemed to find it easier to talk to a complete stranger down an anonymous telephone line than to talk to their own families or friends. Of course in many cases the abuser was a member of the family. I felt that our one little letter to *The Irish Times* had unleashed a torrent that threatened to engulf me. I went to bed each night drained.

Almost all the phone calls were long, often lasting one or two hours. No one can describe a lifetime of suffering in five minutes. We felt honoured by people's trust and deeply upset by their distress. Most people had no intention of appearing in any television programme but just wanted to talk and talk and talk. So we listened and listened and listened. I was acutely conscious that this huge volume of calls represented only the tip of some vast black iceberg of abuse.

Around the middle of the third week the number of calls started to decrease and by the end of that week they had almost stopped. Everybody in the office, even those who didn't take calls, felt as if we had just gone through a huge hurricane of grief. It was impossible not to be affected. It was a long time before I could settle emotionally again.

Having spoken to over a hundred people, we were then faced with the task of making a programme on the basis of what we had heard. Only about twenty of our callers were willing to appear on television. Some of these people were still very distressed and had never been for counselling or therapy. Clearly we could not expose such vulnerable people on screen. In their desperation, their ability to make an informed decision would be blurred and could result in more pain for themselves. They had had enough pain already.

We spent many hours discussing those who were left. We wanted to feel sure that they had come through their abuse and were well on the road to recovery. Above all they needed to be able to articulate their pain and to be reflective about themselves. They needed to describe their journey with honesty and they needed to be strong enough to withstand any repercussions for themselves or their families after the programme. Also they needed to consult their families and have their agreement. Eventually three people emerged, two women and one man – Ruth, Geraldine and Pat. All were willing to be identified.

We made two programmes which were aired in March 1996. After the programmes the three participants had, on the whole, a very positive response. Geraldine said that a bunch of flowers had been left at her door. When she went to collect her children from school some of the other parents had come up to her and just hugged her. Her story appears in this book.

Ruth had found enormous support from her friends, some of whom sat with her whilst the programme was being broadcast. Many others rang later to congratulate her on her bravery and honesty. However, she felt that some people in her local town looked askance at her and tended to avoid her. This she found was very hurtful.

Pat took it all in his stride. He had spoken on television before on the same subject and so was not surprised at people's reactions. He had endless phone calls from other people who had been abused. But he had found the experience of telling his story was a form of catharsis. He now wants to move on. His story appears in these pages also.

So what about all of those who didn't appear on screen? What would happen to their stories?

During the course of those hectic weeks of phone calls I remembered speaking to a woman called Anne. I had listened to her story with a mixture of horror and admiration. Though it was one of the worst abuse stories I had heard, I had been overwhelmed by her strength and "togetherness". I had really hoped that she would agree to appear on our programme but she said very firmly that she wasn't ready. Then in an almost throwaway remark she said quietly "You know girl, you should write a book about all of this."

The more I thought about that suggestion, the more fitting it seemed that some of these stories should be told to a wider audience. In some way this would be a testimony to the courage and strength of the many people who had talked to us and trusted us. They had lived through seemingly insurmountable horrors and yet had survived. In many cases they had not only survived but survived triumphantly and were leading happy and fruitful lives.

Of course there were those who were not doing well. Those who were still victims, and may remain so. Sometimes they remain trapped because they are not yet able for the pain they must face in therapy. Pain frightens us all and to knowingly seek it out can make the stoutest heart quail. When the victim of abuse finally realises that going through the pain is the only way out of it – then there is hope. Therapy is the best option, but no guarantees, no promises!

The stories of many people have not made it onto these pages, simply because the book would have gone on forever. Nonetheless many of their experiences stay with me. I remember Ellen, raped by her father when she was thirteen. He continued to do so for many years afterwards. Now middle-aged she tells me that she is completely bald. She constantly pulls her own hair out by the roots. To hide her self-inflicted baldness she wears a baseball cap all the time. "When you're ugly, you're safe," she says. She lives next door to her father who is now elderly, infirm and living alone. She spends much of her day caring for him.

Then there is Rachel who unwittingly married a paedophile. He seduced her when she was thirteen and as soon as she was old enough he married her. They have several grown-up children. When the children were young Rachel's husband used them to lure other children to their home. There he abused them. It was only when the mother of one of these children told Rachel of what was happening that she had the slightest suspicion of her husband's true nature. She separated from her husband soon afterwards.

James, a priest in his mid-forties, started to have difficulties praying. He found himself becoming more and more distressed and finally sought help in therapy. His initial childhood memories were of loving parents and a father he adored. After a while in therapy some memories started to surface. With the memories came the knowledge that his father had brutally abused him sexually from about the age of seven. The whole town "worshipped" his father who was looked up to by the community. When his father was abusing him James remembers feeling – "I was nothing. I was just a thing."

Dermot, in his mid-thirties, describes himself as "a very unhappy gay man." Both his older brothers abused him regularly and for about two years he was also abused by his mother who he describes as a "raving alcoholic". As a young boy she forced him to masturbate her and perform other sexual acts. To this day he "can't stand the smell of a woman – it makes me feel violently ill." He has been in therapy for a number of years.

There were so many stories and so much pain that it became almost impossible to draw the line somewhere. However, dreadful as the experiences of these people are, they are at least fortunate in one respect – they know they have been abused. This is the first vital step to recovery. Sadly many victims of abuse block out the terrible memories because they are too painful to deal with. This may be an unconscious process, a subconscious method of self preservation.

It seems incredible to many people that traumatic experiences of this nature can be repressed. But as will be seen from the stories that follow, it could be said that repression is the norm rather than the exception. Several victims of abuse have described the tremendous amount of energy that goes into keeping "everything squashed down, and held in." Again this is an unconscious process. The result is often inexplicable depressions, feelings of worthlessness and inadequacy. Almost everybody I spoke to described themselves as feeling unclean and unworthy.

A unique feature of sexual abuse seems to be that it leaves the victims feeling robbed of their spirit, of their souls. They feel their very essence has been taken from them. It is the breaching of their bodily integrity that seems to lead to an intense loss of a sense of one's self.

Commonly, people who have been abused create a new persona for themselves. They put on a mask to face the world just in case anybody should ever get to know the real and "terrible" person underneath. It is a sad fact that those who have been abused usually suffer overwhelming guilt for the abuse – despite the fact that the abuse is not their fault. Invariably the abuser makes his or her victim feel a huge sense of shame. Survivors of abuse describe themselves as "bad people".

To counteract their deep sense of inner ugliness many survivors develop all sorts of survival mechanisms. They can become totally introverted and withdrawn or go to the opposite extreme and become the life and soul of the party. Often good actors, they can create an impression of supreme self-confidence and many become very high achievers, filling their lives with all sorts of activity. A number of survivors have described themselves to me as "living a life on the run."

Almost inevitably the running has to stop sometime. It would seem that this can happen in all sorts of ways – a breakdown, severe depression, problems with relationships, alcoholism, drug addiction and many more.

At this stage help is essential. But where do you go

for help and what kind of help is available? I have included a list at the end of this book of some contact numbers. However, a number of people I spoke to had received very little help. Sometimes this was because they simply did not know where to go. All of the Rape Crisis Centres throughout Ireland offer counselling to those who have been sexually abused. Most of them will offer help to men and women but waiting lists can be long, often stretching for several months or more. To those who have recently realised that they have been sexually abused this wait may impose an extra intolerable strain.

Many of the health boards around the country also offer help but again there might be waiting lists. Your doctor can also refer you to a local hospital for psychiatric help. If all of these avenues fail there is always the alternative of seeking help privately. This can be expensive but many people who have gone this route say that it is the best money they have ever spent. But a word of warning for anybody seeking help, private or public – not all therapists are equally skilled.

Inevitably there will be people who are good at this job and those who are not. One young woman who contacted us, described her visit to a consultant psychiatrist in a large city hospital. Lucy's memories of her abuse had finally surfaced and she had been as she describes it herself "climbing the walls" in her distress. She described her symptoms and explained her background to the psychiatrist who listened attentively and then said "Well that's all in the past now, you must just put it behind you and move on." She felt as if she had been kicked in the teeth. However, as you will see from some of the stories that follow, other people have felt that their sanity was saved by a kind and caring psychiatrist.

There are many different types of counsellors and therapists and it can take time to find the right person for you. Sometimes people go to a recommended therapist and counsellor and feel very unhappy with the help they get. They are then afraid to try again. Different counsellors work for different people. Ask around and get recommendations from friends or other professionals. Do not be put off by an unsatisfactory experience – keep looking until you find the right person for you.

Because people who have been abused usually have a very poor self-image they may mistrust their own judgement. Because of their lack of self-confidence they may feel unable to say "no" to someone who has been recommended to them. It is important to remember that this is your life and you are entitled to seek the best possible help that you can find.

There are no promises, but there is hope.

GERALDINE

GERALDINE

"I don't think I ever really slept for all those years."

She is tall and dark haired and wears a loose, deep-pink shirt. Her voice is gentle and there is a sense of calmness and stillness about her. We sit and talk in her warm yellow sitting room. We arrange to meet in the evening when her children are in bed. She is now in her early thirties and she and her husband are expecting their third child.

There were two periods of abuse in my life and I've always been conscious of the second period because I was of an age where I knew it was wrong. I was a teenager and I had a better idea about the physical side of life and sex. In both cases the abusers were my brothers.

I have three brothers and from about the age of fourteen onwards my second eldest brother Joe abused me. I remember it was the weekend after my eldest brother's wedding and I woke up one night and Joe was at me. He had pulled my blankets down and he was touching me and feeling me. As I would push him away with one hand he was feeling with another. I was telling him to go away and leave me alone and I could smell an awful lot of drink on his breath. He has a very violent temper, and if drink is taken it's twice as bad.

He was twenty-six at the time and I was fourteen, the youngest in the family. I was at home in my own bedroom. I shared with my sister, but by this stage she wasn't living at home. I kept saying to him "go away or I'll get Mammy." There was no response and he certainly wasn't leaving. We had bunk beds and I was in the top bunk and I literally just jumped out of the bed and ran in for my mother. I woke her and told her that Joe was in my room and he had no clothes on, he was touching me and he wouldn't leave me alone.

I knew she was due to go into hospital the following week for treatment for her arthritis. I was terribly upset at this stage and when I woke her she said "go away, go back into your room, how can you possibly expect me to go into hospital while you're carrying on like this?" She told me not to make a scene and to keep quiet and not wake my Dad who was in the bed beside her. Then she said I wasn't to tell anyone about it. My Dad didn't wake up, I'd say he had a few drinks on him and was just in a very deep sleep – or so I used to think.

Afterwards I always used to ask myself "why the hell didn't I wake him up that night as opposed to her and he would have done something about it?" But knowing what I know now I just can't possibly accept that any more.

By the time I got back into my room Joe was gone. I don't really remember very much about the rest of the night other than the fact that I didn't sleep very well. I kept waiting for him to come back but he didn't that night. That was really the story of my life until I got married when I was just twenty two. Just as it had started without warning, it also finished without warning when I was about seventeen or eighteen. But I never knew when it would end, so anytime I was in the house on my own with Joe there was always this unease and the expectation that something might happen.

After that first night there were many more nights like that. After the second or third time I decided it was safer to sleep in the bottom bunk because I felt that when I was in the top bunk I was at his level because he's tall. I thought that being in the bottom bunk was like a safety alarm because he would have to kneel down and I might hear him. I found that if I woke up and found he was there it was awful.

The big joke in our house was "Geraldine's bedroom". My room was constantly a mess, always around the door area. The rest of the room was very tidy but when you walked into my bedroom the area around the door was always cluttered. You could trip over things and break your neck – but it made noise. I was trying to set up an early alarm system. We weren't allowed locks on our doors. I asked for a key but I was told "oh we have no use for keys in this house." The whole ethos of our house was that we had nothing to hide from ourselves, nothing to fear from ourselves, it was always outsiders. We were never to trust outsiders. Even though no outsider ever hurt me it was something I grew up with and took a long time to get over. There was always this idea that the family would club together and the outside world was a bad place.

I used to leave the light on in my room as well because I did study hard. If the light was on he might think I was still awake and he wouldn't come in. He would only come in the safety of knowing I was asleep. Sometimes I would also leave a little radio on, because then he might think that if the radio was on I was listening to music. I started to sleep in a sleeping bag because I discovered that blankets could be pulled off. I used to have the zip part of the sleeping bag against the wall and a blanket over it, thinking it was safe.

I slept with my hockey stick under the bed where it was easier to reach than in the top bunk. I used the hockey stick to hit him – anything to push him away. I don't think I ever actually hit him with the hockey stick, even though it was there. It was just something that gave me peace of mind. I don't think I ever really went asleep for all those years. I have this strong memory that my first full night's deep sleep of safety was my wedding night. I remember waking up the next morning and saying to Des, my husband, "I know it's an awful thing to say but that was the best night's sleep I ever had in my life". It was because I felt so safe.

She laughs at the memory.

Because we had no locks on any of the doors when I was going up to have a bath I'd have to make a big, major announcement, " I'm going up for a bath." But that was like issuing an invitation because he would invariably open the door or walk in and say "sorry". In the bathroom we had a big, heavy medicine cabinet and I used to move it against the bathroom door. It was one of those old fashioned cabinets that rested on the floor. There were numerous times he did things like that, usually involving touching and feeling.

I think I always used to blame it on his drinking – he

wasn't doing it on purpose to me. Obviously I've learnt differently since then. The abuse itself was probably not the worst – the worst was the way my mother had turned away from me and that made me feel that I had done something wrong.

She pauses and closes her eyes for a moment.

My other brother Frank at that stage had started going out with his future wife and she used to stay weekends with us. It was such a pain in the neck, she stayed Friday and Saturday night in my room. Monday to Friday there was school or work and I used to look forward to the weekends to relax but I was never given that opportunity. But equally I knew the nights she was there I was safe, so it worked well from that point of view.

When I was sixteen my Dad got very ill and he died when I was seventeen. It was a very confusing time for me. I never, ever spoke to my Dad about the abuse. I find it hard now to believe that he didn't know something was going on – whether it was abuse or whether it was Joe trying to hit me. Because I made noise. It wasn't a case of "Joe please go away", I was ranting and raving and shouting in the night and nobody came. Nobody came ever, even when I was screaming the place down. I used to think that because my Dad was a heavy drinker he was just in a drunken stupor. But now I just can't accept that he was always drunk. At the time it was that belief that kept me going. I believed that if he knew what was going on he'd stop it. I had to hold onto that thought and that's what got me through in those days.

Looking back on that period of abuse I realise that it isolated me from people I liked or people I trusted. In secondary school I had three very close friends, one in particular. When the abuse started I pulled myself away from them in fear that they would ever find out about me. Because of the reaction from my Mum I was just so afraid that everybody would react that way. I cut myself off and the sad part is I've lost contact with these friends because of it.

I always did very well in school. Because of the way my mother had treated me by turning me away I felt I had done something wrong and that I needed to make up for it. From that moment on, until I started my counselling for abuse, I spent the rest of my life trying to make up to my mother. At that time the only thing I could do was to be brilliant at school. I worked very, very hard and got no acknowledgement for it whatsoever. I did the best of all my family, but all I ever heard about was how well my brothers had done. When I studied very hard the attitude was "she must be thick if she has to work that hard."

She sighs. She grimaces slightly and her hands clench briefly.

At that time I had wanted to do law and I got enough points in my Leaving Certificate to do it. My Dad had worked in the university and so I would have had free tuition even though he was dead at this stage. My mother wouldn't have had to pay for it. But for some reason I felt this awful compulsion that I had to go out and work to earn money to give to my mother.

So I didn't go to college. It's a decision I regret now. I did a secretarial course which I hated. I'd liked school and I never once bunked off school but I used to think of every excuse I could to get out of going to the secretarial course. I absolutely hated it. But my mother had done a secretarial course so if it was good enough for her, it was good enough for me. Then I got the job that I still work in today.

When I got the job I did think now and then of moving out from home, particularly when things got difficult at home for other reasons. Joe was always the cause of trouble in our house. My mother would always accuse us of ganging up on him. There's a huge age range in our family so at no point were we all friends together. There were numerous huge rows between him and one of my other brothers and people would take sides. There were times when it was really very uncomfortable.

Our house was always on edge when Joe was around. Even when he was in his middle to late twenties it was still our responsibility to make sure he went to work on time. We had no timer on the immersion and my mother would get out of bed at six o'clock in the morning to switch on the immersion heater so that the water would be warm for Joe. She wouldn't do this for anybody else. This hot water was just for Joe. Even though he wouldn't get up on time, and was always late, we weren't allowed to use the hot water and we would have been up for hours before him.

Eventually he would storm down the stairs at about nine o'clock and my mother would have his breakfast waiting for him. If you looked crooked at him, almighty war could break out, and it was always our fault, never his fault. He was menacing and he had a violent temper. I don't know how many times we had to get a plasterer in to the house because he'd banged his hand through a wall or he'd broken door handles.

I'm too young to remember but there are famous, or infamous, stories in our house about him and my other two brothers fighting and having split heads and cut arms. I do remember himself and my Dad having actual fisticuffs. He also hit my sister and he's hit me.

He still lives at home with my mother and he's now in his forties. When she was well enough she was still running around to the butcher's to get him his favourite bit of steak and his fish on a Friday. She'd be doing his ironing and making sure his suit went to the right dry cleaners.

When I was about seventeen or eighteen Joe stopped abusing me. By this time he had had some girlfriends. I remember a night when he tried to rape one of his girlfriends and I stopped him. She was staying in the house in my room and he was trying it on with her very strongly and I jumped out of the bed and ordered him out of the room. She was one of the few of Joe's girlfriends that we were all very fond of. She was lovely, but from that day on I always felt very awkward when I was in her company because I felt guilt by association. He was my brother and he had done this to her.

When I was eighteen I met Des and we were very attracted to each other and became close friends. We got married when I was still very young for all the wrong reasons, although I didn't realise it at the time. It's only on reflection and through counselling that I realised that really my marriage was my only escape out of the house. It in turn caused other problems in relation to our marriage.

Even after we had two children I still had this terrible

need to make up to my mother, and although my brother was living at home, it was always me who brought her shopping, cut the hedge and did the grass.

After some time we were having severe difficulties in our marriage, but it wasn't until we hit rock bottom and were on the point of separation that we went for marriage counselling. We did two weeks and it was horrendous. Then we did the next six weeks and things seemed to be going back. Then, I think it was in week seven, that the "S" word was mentioned, sex in general, and I just froze. Although I had always known about Joe's abuse I hadn't really spoken to anyone about it. Des knew about Joe in the sense that I used to say "I think I was molested". I just barely mentioned it and then I'd say to myself "it's okay now" and I'd just push it aside. I knew full well what had happened but I felt so dirty that I wasn't even able to tell Des all about it. It was years of counselling before I could say the word "abuse".

She pauses to take several deep breaths.

During week seven we came to physical sexuality in general and I just died a death. I knew there was no escape and I was going to have to talk about Joe. I came home and I said to Des "you know, I'm really going to have to bring this up." I really felt that it was going to be a shameful thing for me and Des to have to bring it up in our sessions. I was looking for his permission to do it, because I'd never had permission from anybody else. We dithered a bit about how we should say it but then Des put me on the spot when he went for our next session. He said to our counsellor "when Geraldine comes in to you the next day there is something she needs to talk to you about, and I don't think she will."

So when I arrived the next day I knew I had to tell the counsellor and there was no escape. So the whole story of Joe came out. When I described what had happened it was all very vague and I was saying things like "I think he touched me here and I think he touched me there". Then the counsellor said the word "abuse" and I nearly died. I was ready to fight with him. I wasn't "abused". I remember coming out of the session and thinking "I have told all about this and now it's all over – phew, what do I do now?" Little did I know at that stage I'd only scratched the surface.

The sessions continued for another few weeks and my counsellor gave me a book called *Surviving Sexual Abuse* by Rosemary Liddy. It's geared to any age group but especially for teenagers. It's very simplistic and very easy to read in one sense, but it was the most difficult book I ever read.

I came back home and Des was working in the spare room. I thought "grand, into bed, read a book, no problem." So I got in and was reading this book and before I knew it I was in the study with Des, roaring crying, in a horrendous state. I was shaking with blinding headaches. They were so bad that they were like visions of light coming to the centre of my head. I don't remember much about it . . .

She stops again briefly, a look of distress on her face.

. . . but Des tells me all I kept saying was "oh God no, please God don't let it be true, please God don't let it be true!" I remember saying to Des "I'm not sure what happened but Frank did something", and from that moment on my world literally fell apart.

All the memories came flooding back of an earlier period of abuse by a brother who, in later life, I had trusted so completely. He was the person I turned to when my father was ill. He was the person I trusted so much that we made him godfather to one of our children, a decision I regret terribly now. But that's how deeply I had buried the memories.

Her voice trembles as she remembers the next bit.

By the end of the night I had remembered a lot. I'd go asleep and the next minute I'd wake up and go "Jesus Christ! No, not that." Over the next couple of weeks the flashes would come very quickly and I'd try to push them away. Then they would came back more vividly and the memories would be clearer and clearer. I found myself saying "oh God no that didn't really happen! Because I was so young I'm confusing it. Because I'm dealing with Joe I'm getting totally confused." But the memories would come back clearer and clearer and I could even remember what I was wearing and where I was. Everything came back so strongly that I knew it was true.

The earliest memories were when I was about five or six. My Mum had to go out to work for a period of about six years. She didn't get home until about four o'clock in the afternoon. Frank, who's six years older than me, is the youngest of my three brothers. We were the only ones in the family still going to primary school. I was very dependent on him when I came home. I needed him to let me in, but he became so untrustworthy as regards being late and losing keys that in the end I was given the keys. I was also dependent on him to light the gas. Even today I'm still terrified of matches and gas cookers. On cold days when we came in from school I used to drink cocoa, it was the only hot drink I took. I needed him to light the gas. It sounds very simplistic now, but that's how the power struggle started.

He'd say "I won't be home to let you in unless you do something for me." In the beginning he'd get me to do his jobs for him. He'd say "you do the washing up for me and do this for me and that for me." But gradually it all changed. I think it was when he was becoming more adolescent, maybe ten or eleven, and I was about five.

We had a garage and my Dad was a mechanic and so there was always a very strong smell of engine oil in the garage. It was a very dark place and I was never comfortable in it. I always had the impression that it was rat-infested and crawling with spiders. In fact it wasn't, but that was the impression I had. Frank used to terrify me with stories saying there were people buried under the floor and things like that. I still have a terrible fear of the unknown and horror movies.

He used to really scare the living daylights out of me. If I had to go out to the garage for something he'd come out and he'd stand between me and the door back into the kitchen and tell me horror stories about death or spiders or aliens or darkness. I was five or six and I believed every word he told me because he was so much older than me. He was the only one who had time for me, or so I thought. I used to think that he was the only one there to protect me.

My Mum used to always go to her Mum on a Saturday evening. My mother honestly thought that up until the day he died that my Dad used to stay at home with us every Saturday night. But he always used to go around to the pub. He was always home by half-ten or eleven to collect her. She used to ring to say when she was ready to be collected. If he wasn't home when she rang we used to always lie and say "he's up in the loo, we'll tell him to go and get you when he comes down." Somebody would run around to the pub and tell him he had to go for her now. We weren't supposed to be allowed out on a Saturday night but Daddy always let us go out and play.

Often my older sister would be baby-sitting and my two older brothers would be gone out so Frank and I would be left in the house together. In fairness to my mother she probably thought I was in bed by ten o'clock on a Saturday night but little did she know that I used to run up to bed when I heard the car coming into the drive.

She laughs.

So I actually spent an awful lot of time alone with Frank. He had complete and utter control over me. He started putting me down from day one. There was always this implication that he was superior to me in every way. Not only was he really superior but I was really stupid and thick and I couldn't do anything right. I wasn't to be listened to and whatever I said wasn't taken with any validity. There was this idea that I was only a mere female. I always felt that I had to do what he said because he knew best.

Slowly it started to change. He started to introduce this idea of the physical and bodies and the difference between men and women. He showed me pornographic pictures. I don't know where he got them, he was only ten or eleven. Maybe they belonged to my older brothers, but I really don't know. But that's where it started.

I remember one night he used the word "penis" and I thought it was the funniest word I'd ever heard in my life. It had always been referred to in our house as "willy". So when he used this word I didn't know what it was. Then he showed me his penis, and it was erect, and I was really scared because I didn't know what it was – to me it was like a giant mushroom. I didn't know what to say. From then on it got much, much more physical.

This all built up over a period of time until I was about nine or ten. Physically I had started to develop very early so I had boobs by the age of ten and he started to feel them. He was about fifteen or sixteen. I often remember lying on my tummy out in the back garden and he'd come over and lie down beside me and he'd slip his hand in where it couldn't be seen. Of course I couldn't move or turn. Even though I wasn't sexually aware I didn't like the idea of people thinking that he was touching me.

She pauses as she searches for the right words.

I can't explain that, but I just felt uncomfortable. I felt that somebody might see. I think I was uncomfortable at the sense of sexuality about it. I was at a very difficult age, the facts of life and sex weren't explained to me at all.

All of a sudden I had these boobs I didn't know where they were coming from. Then I suddenly seemed to be getting a different sort of attention from Frank and it wasn't an attention I liked. I remember talking to my sister and saying "when I grow up I'm going to cut my boobies off, I don't want to be a woman, I don't want to have these boobies, I don't want all this." She used to laugh at me but I never went into it any further with her.

It was Frank's attention during that period, which is obviously a very difficult time for any girl, that put me off the idea of being a woman at all. I remember I ate and put on a huge amount of weight. I thought that if I made all my body fat I wouldn't have these boobs. But it didn't work that way, I was left with a lot of weight and feeling very awkward anyway.

One night he made me hold his penis and I was really scared by this. I was not happy with this at all. I did say something to my sister. I couldn't remember the word "penis" it made me just crack up laughing so I said "Frank made me hold his pyramid." She obviously said something to him. I don't know what. But he went from being the only person in my life to being nothing. He totally withdrew from me and was absolutely horrible and obnoxious to me. He was actually mean to me.

I remember we were walking to evening Mass one Sunday and my Dad was just a little bit ahead of us. I said to Frank "why aren't you my friend any more?" He said "no, it's you who's not my friend." Then I said "but you don't talk to me." He said "I don't talk to you any more because you tell everything I say." This was his thing, I was his special friend and I shouldn't have told.

So of course, big eejit that I am, I said "sorry, please

be my friend" and he said we'd talk about it when we got home from Mass. The talk about it when we came home from Mass ended up with me being raped on the landing that Sunday evening.

Everybody was downstairs watching *The Riordans*. I was nine or ten, he was sixteen, and he raped me.

Once more we must pause. Geraldine draws a few deep breaths and looks down at her hands.

He hadn't done anything like that before. It went from being kind of innocent to a very, very sexual, vicious attack. I don't really know how it happened, I don't know how it got that far. I can remember the pain. The pain of penetration was so severe and I actually felt that my eyes were bulging out of my head. That's a very strong, vivid memory. It seemed to me that the more the pain was etched on my face the more enjoyment he was deriving from it. I've always had this very strong impression of his face, when I've had nightmares. He had this dark, jet black hair and very pale complexion. But I always saw his eyes.

I remember my counsellor got me to draw what I could remember of the rape and he actually was stunned by my portrayal of these eyes. They were just dark and full of evil. I can't draw but in the picture I did for him he was shocked by what I had done to the eyes. That was the way I always remembered it. For a long time as a result of that I always had this fear of confrontation because those eyes were stronger than me. Those eyes had everything in them, from his physical power to his perceived intellectual superiority to me.

I didn't scream.

Again she breathes deeply.

I don't know why. The pain was horrendous, but I think that he told me to stay quiet.

Then we heard somebody coming up the stairs and there was a huge kerfuffle to get away. I knew it was wrong and I had to jump up to make everything okay. It's ironic now, looking back, but it was actually Joe who came up the stairs. He didn't catch us or anything but I'm sure we had very guilty expressions on our faces. He just gave us a look. I can't explain the look either.

I remember going into my room and my sister wasn't there and being absolutely stunned by the whole thing. Not really realising at that stage what had happened, but knowing that it was wrong. I think it was more from the point of view that if somebody liked you as much as he said he liked me it shouldn't hurt that much. It was just the fear of the unknown and the pain. It was really, really very sore. I could feel myself shrinking. I didn't know these words at the time and that's not an expression I would have used then but looking back on it that's the way I felt. I felt I was shrinking on the inside.

I knew not to tell anyone and I didn't.

Then a few weeks later in school I remember somebody in class saying this girl was seen kissing her brother the other day. The whole class's reaction was "yuck!" At that stage I just wanted the whole world to swallow me up. Because I thought, well, if they think that about her what are they going to say about me? I realised then how wrong it was. I had good friends and I withdrew from them. These were friends that I used to stay with and we really were very, very close. Even though I stayed in their houses they never stayed in mine. Looking back on it now I always felt safer staying in their houses. In one friend's house I remember always wishing that her father was my father. I always wanted to belong to her family. It always felt so safe. It just seemed easier.

I think I was afraid to invite a friend to stay because I remember one time a cousin of mine stayed with us for a night. I remember the next day she said to me "Joe was in our room last night and he was naked and you told him to go away." I said to her "no, he wasn't, you must have been dreaming." But he was.

After the rape on the landing I was injured. There was blood in my urine the next day and I was brought to the doctor. It was just diagnosed as a kidney infection. I think the doctor just took a sample of my urine but she didn't examine me. During the time that Joe was abusing me I had recurrent cystitis, but that was more from anxiety than anything else. The doctor never questioned me or anything like that. I sometimes think she should have noticed these things, but I don't know if that's fair.

I was certainly very sore for a few days afterwards and I think I just went very quiet. Frank didn't say anything to me. From that moment on I deliberately tried to put myself out of his reach. I didn't want to be in his company. I kept making sure that if I was in his company there was somebody else there. If I was in the back garden and he came over near me I moved away before he got to me. That was certainly the end of his abuse. But he still tried to make moves on me and I always moved away. At some stage it just ended. I don't know when, but it just ended. I still remembered it but over the years I slowly pushed the memory away. There were other things going on.

When Frank started going out with his wife, I remember the first time I met her thinking "God, if she knew!" And from that moment on it was all totally forgotten. I never told anybody, ever.

Frank's abuse ruined my body image. I'm heavy now, but I was very, very slim then. My boobs were always the biggest part of me and I hated them, even when I was married. I was left feeling uncomfortable with being a woman. I think Frank damaged my physical image and Joe and my mother did the mental and emotional damage. I'm sure there's overlapping between them, but that's the way I divide the two.

I absolutely hated myself and I didn't understand why. When I looked in the mirror I saw myself as heavy even when I was thin. I could show you photographs where I was nearly anorexic looking, you could count the bones in my face. I was very conscious of my weight. I didn't like what I saw. It was obviously the inside I didn't like.

In relation to Joe and my mother I always felt I had done something wrong and I always had this making up to do. This turned out to be a big problem in our marriage because when things weren't always my fault I was always very quick to accept the blame. It became very easy for Des to say "it was your fault and you did this and that." I would accept it without question because I just automatically thought I was always in the wrong. I never stood up for myself in work or in arguments because I just didn't think I had the right to do that.

In a strange way I was very closed to the world and to people. As a trained counsellor would say, I "role-played" and I was very good at it. I really like the place where I work, we call it one big happy family, and I suppose it is in many ways. There's a huge amount of sexual innuendo, but it's all very light and very open and there's nothing mischievous or nasty about it. I suppose it was the first place that I felt comfortable in that way. I could double-talk with the best of them. As a result nobody would have had an iota that it was the hardest thing I was doing. It was never to let anyone think that I had a problem with this. I fooled the world. Very few people got to know the real me, and in fact I don't think anyone did. That was where the problems came into the marriage. Des thought he was marrying somebody different than I turned out to be.

I was acting. I would show a hint of feeling or emotion but never too much. Again that goes back to my Mum. I remember at my Dad's funeral when he was being buried I was roaring crying and I got into trouble for that. It was okay to cry a little but not to make a scene. So you were allowed to have the emotion but with decorum. I developed this protective cocoon around myself. I had to stay closed, it was the only way to protect myself from any sort of hurt or pain.

I didn't totally block off all emotions and feelings, but they were measured and they were rationalised. I would allow myself so much feeling in this direction or that direction and then I closed off. I showed enough to get by. I was very fortunate that Des, though he's changed through counselling, would have been kind of a closed-off person also. He was happy enough to remain closed-off, so it didn't encourage an awful lot of openness in me. Every now and then we overlapped and that was it.

When I was growing up our family was a family of secrets. The left hand never knew what the right hand was doing. I understand there's a certain amount of privacy needed in every family and there are some things you don't discuss outside. That's fair enough and normal and right. But nothing of ours was ever discussed. I mean, if we were getting a new carpet, it was "don't say it outside." Even the good things were kept secret in our house. My mother would tell somebody something and say "don't tell your sister. Don't tell your brother." She'd be saying the same to the other brother or sister. She played us off against one another very skilfully, to keep us apart so that we would never get close enough to talk about what was really going on.

My mother placed huge emphasis on physical appearance and I was always hearing about my great sister and her wonderful job and how beautiful and thin she was. My bad body image was totally reinforced by my mother.

When relatives visited us it was always a great source of pride to my mother that they had no "dirt" on us. At this stage a few of my cousins had had babies out of wedlock, and one had been in trouble with the police. My mother always took great pride in looking down on these people whilst nobody could say a bad word about us. Whereas the truth of it was that Joe was in serious trouble with the police, yet he never had to pay the consequences for anything he ever did. Strings were always pulled – big time. It was mainly my father who pulled the strings because he was put under huge pressure from my Mum.

I now recognise that she's an evil woman and a bigot. I used to make excuses for her. Then when I became a mother myself and we had huge problems in our marriage I still knew that there was no way that I'd have allowed the things to go on in my house that used to go on in our house. Even through all our difficulties, Des and I never hid anything from the children. Nothing is a secret in our house, at all – nothing. Maybe there are things that should be secrets, but we just don't believe in that at all.

As a mother I don't know how you could have a favourite child. You might love a particular attribute of one child more in that child than in the other but in the end it evens out. I remember when our second baby was born our older child was still very much a baby. In hospital the night before we were due to come home with him I was crying my heart out to Des "what have we done? We're never going to be able to love another baby." I thought that the love was going to be divided, but as soon as the new baby came home it was multiplied. And that was always the way it was going to be.

I've no idea why my mother was the way she was. That's the million dollar question. I don't know why she did what she did. I don't know why she has always stood by Joe as opposed to any of the others. Maybe there were problems in her own family.

When I was in counselling I went to see my mother and tried to bring the conversation around to what had happened me as a child. But she pushed the conversation away and there were tears on both sides, guilt induced. I felt like I was the worst daughter in the world because I'd upset her so much. Eventually my counsellor said to me "Geraldine, you are going to confront her. You're not going to hear if and why, you are going down there to tell her what happened. You're not going down there for an excuse, you're not going down there for her to turn it around. You are going to take control of the situation and you are going down to say that this is what happened." That was easier said than done.

I had always noticed when our first child was born, and she was a girl, my mother doted on her. I felt she was making up to me through my daughter and thought I could cope with that. Then our son was born and I saw the pattern starting again. Here was a wonderful boy. My mother turned it into a male/female thing and all of a sudden my daughter was pushed to one side. I remember one weekend it was my daughter's birthday and my mother got her a little present but got my son a much bigger one. Even though he was only two or three at the time he went around the house like Mister Big Head and my poor daughter was very deflated. In that microcosm of a weekend I could see how Joe was created.

I often refer to Joe as "Frankenstein's monster" because he was created. He became the person that he is because he was allowed to. My mother couldn't have stopped Joe abusing me that first night but she could have stopped what happened from then on – but she didn't. I saw her doing the same thing with my children as she had done with us and what I couldn't do for myself I could do for my children.

She sounds really angry for the first time.

I think it was at that moment that I knew I was a different mother to her. I went straight in to her and I said "how dare you. Don't start your dangerous games with my children." She just looked at me and I just let fly. I said "I've had years of that. I won't have my daughter go through what I went through." Then the whole thing about the abuse came up. I didn't give her a chance to turn on the guilt trip. I wouldn't allow it to happen.

She sat there and nodded. She didn't actually admit anything but skilfully played the game and said she hadn't known about what happened to me. When I confronted her she didn't not accept it. She didn't deny it. She just didn't really say anything – which is unlike her. I said that neither I nor my children would ever come here again and she wasn't welcome in our family. She didn't try and do anything to stop it – and I left. I haven't been back to see her.

By this time I was talking about abuse relatively freely in my sessions and I thought this was great. But my counsellor said I was never going to get over it until I confronted my brothers. I think many people who go through counselling hear this thing of "you have to feel the pain." And you sit there and you think "it's so easy for him to say that. He hasn't a clue what pain is about." My anger used to be nearly targeted at him and I used to say "you just don't know what it's like!" But having gone through it and come out the other side, unfortunately you do have to go back there. You have to go back and feel the pain because it's only by feeling the pain you make it real again and by making it real you have to deal with it.

It's not good enough to say I know what happened and that's it. That person is always going to have that power over your life. It's like the way I always had this image of Frank's eyes. I was always physically afraid of Joe – but I think I could floor Joe now. I wouldn't hold back and Frank doesn't scare me any more, but that's only because I've confronted them.

I had been building up to confronting Joe. It all sounds very easy now but in between those periods of confrontation there was deep despair, deep darkness, panic attacks, terrible self-doubt, suicidal thoughts. Having spoken about the abuse but still not feeling any better – the marriage still going nowhere, life was miserable. I felt I'd spoken about this, so why didn't I feel any better?

My counsellor kept bringing me back to the point that it all builds up inside you and it either comes to a stage where you totally hate yourself and all you want to do is kill yourself, or you just have to let go. You have to confront. My brothers who had abused me were becoming more and more powerful, even though I was older now and knew what had happened. I couldn't take it any more. I really was close to cracking up.

I love to write. I can really let go in my writing and I can really understand my feelings. What I can't always understand in my mind I can understand in my writing. I'm not an angry person by nature, I think maybe that has been at times to my detriment.

It was a Friday evening and I could just feel myself getting angry. So I sat at the computer and before I realised it I had written a letter to Joe. It was all about the abuse. Without actually consciously sitting down to write it that's what came out. I said "well, feck it anyway – I'm going down with it and I'm going to tell him. I'm not just going to hand a letter in, he's going to face me." I was shaking like a leaf at this stage and I rang Des and asked him if he could come home from work just a little bit early that day.

I explained to him what I'd written and he said "oh God!' He didn't know what was going to happen. So we went down to my mother's and I rang the doorbell and Joe opened the door. My mother came thundering down the stairs and I said "right, you just stop there now. I'm actually delighted you're here, because you're going to hear what I have to say to him so none of you can say you didn't know." I told him I was giving him this letter about how he had abused me and the awful effect he'd had on my life. I stared him in the eye and he couldn't look at me. His head kept going down all the time and I kept telling him "you look at me when I'm speaking to you." I was invited to step in and I said "I will not go into a house with you two here, I will not close the door behind me, I don't trust either of you." I spoke on the doorstep and I was nearly hoping the neighbours would come out. I gave it all back to him and in front of my mother, and it was also in writing.

He didn't say anything and I didn't want him to say anything. I wasn't there to listen. I was there to tell my story and that was the way I dealt with it. I turned around and I walked away, I didn't run away. I walked down that drive with my head held high for the first time and got into the car. Although I was shaking and nervous I felt powerful, I really felt powerful for the first time.

Before this if I ever saw my mother or brother when I was out walking I'd have been dodging behind hedges and walls in fear. A couple of months ago I literally physically bumped into him in a shop and I just thought it was hilarious. I didn't do anything, it didn't bother me. I didn't acknowledge him.

I know that it's silence that condemns the next generation to abuse so I decided to confront Frank but not in the same way. He works away from home and I don't always know when he's there. Quite by chance I heard he was home and that he was going away to work the following Friday. So I rang him and I spoke to him in much the same way I'd spoken to Joe. I finished by saying "if I ever hear anything ever happens to your children, you're dead." He hung up at that point.

I had told him exactly what he had done to me including the rape. I said to myself "he is not getting off this easy." I wrote him a letter as well and then I drove out to his house on my own and put it into the letter box. The house was in absolute darkness. I was very concerned for his wife and children. I didn't want to upset their lives. As much as I wanted to protect his children, I didn't want to cause unnecessary hurt. Little did I know that she already knew about the things that Frank had done. My other sister-in-law had already said it to her some months before. I don't know whether she believes it or not.

My feelings for my father have changed through all this. He was my hero that never existed, my hero who never had to do anything. "If only I had gone to Daddy it would all have been different." I know now it wouldn't have been different. There is no way on God's earth I can honestly say that every night when Joe tried to abuse me Daddy was in a drunken stupor. That wouldn't be true.

I don't know why he did nothing. I've never been able to fully answer that question. He was a man with a violent temper, like Joe, a man who when he drank pints was wonderful and when he drank whiskey he was the devil. In the six months before he died, things had eased and my mother and he had become quite close. But the two years prior to that were a nightmare. He was drinking very heavily and so was she. They were fighting all the time and it was dreadful. That memory had been pushed aside when he became ill. You see he changed when he became ill. He became a very gentle person and I thought "isn't he lovely". I didn't realise that he had to change because he was dependent on me and my Mum. He was brought home, we didn't leave him in hospital.

Everything sounds wonderful for me now but there were terrible dark moments. I think the worst time was the realisation that there was a severe problem and that because of what happened not only my life but my husband's life, and possibly my children's lives, had been ruined. I felt powerless to change it. Des and I did actually separate for a period of time. Everything was just getting worse and worse. I really didn't think I was going to make it.

I felt because I had been abused it was as if I had it tattooed across my forehead – "I have been raped. I am dirty." It wasn't really a topic for coffee break in work and there was nowhere to turn. It was a very, very lonely and difficult time. Through all of this and my marriage difficulties I had a very close friend in work and she has been very good. She saved my life. But apart from her, despite our difficulties, Des was the only one who listened. Even when we were living apart he was the one who would listen.

Purely by chance we've ended up with the best counselling possible. It has been a huge financial burden. We reckon that we must have spent £25,000 to £30,000 at this stage and it was worth every penny and more. I feel there should be government-funded help for counselling for abuse. There should also be tax relief on it because it's very very expensive and it's not covered under VHI. If we hadn't been able to afford counselling then we'd have had to wait for one of the State agency counsellors and drain the Exchequer of its money that way. Or we could have separated and we'd have to be claiming all sorts of allowances. So even at the bare minimum there should be tax relief on counselling.

Today things are so completely different. I'm not quite finished therapy yet but I'm certainly in the last stages. It has been slowed up because I'm pregnant, which in itself is an answer to the abuse. I don't know how we conceived our other two children with all of this going on, but this baby has been conceived in total love. I would hate for our other two children to think they weren't loved because they are, very much – but their conception was very much more of a physical act than an act of love. There are nothing but good feelings associated with this baby. For me it's like the final answer to the abuse. It's the final ray of hope. I've been to hell and beyond. Not only have I come back, but now I'm heading in the other direction.

The world has opened up. I'm not afraid to be me any more. Most of the time I even like me. The darker moments are there from time to time and I think that's okay. I think people who have been abused have an expectation of perfection and that's where they go wrong. We expect Utopia and other people can't deliver that and that's the reason we stay closed off. I know life isn't perfect and I don't expect it to be perfect. Now I'm able to cope with imperfections and problems – every time a problem comes up and I cope with it, I think that's another victory for me, that's another time that the abuse goes further and further into the past.

It is in the past. It never ever goes away but it has less and less of an impact on our lives. The only impact it has now is a positive one. It was very difficult to trust again. To open up emotionally. The physical side of our marriage was difficult, but now it isn't. If there are difficulties I don't run away from them any more. I don't feel guilty, I don't feel dirty. It's something to be spoken about. I often think now that our marriage is probably stronger than that of an awful lot of people I know.

I look to the future with hope. I don't fear the future. I'm not caught in the past where I was. My future was always back in the past. Now I look to the future. The world is my oyster. I feel like a lot of years have been wasted in many respects. These are years I can never regain. After my baby is born I hope to go back studying, at some stage I know I will. It mightn't be this year or next year, but I know I will. Anything is possible and that's the joy of it.

PAT

PAT

"I was the last boy to officially leave Artane in 1969."

Deeply tanned from working outdoors, he has a warm and ready smile. In his early forties, he is fit and vigorous. His face bears the marks of many old scars. A year ago he moved from an overcrowded Dublin suburb and now lives in the West of Ireland with his wife and children.

He drives to Dublin and we meet outside a nearby pub. He follows me in his car back to my house. We sit down with cups of coffee and he lights a cigarette.

(Some of the names in this story have been changed to protect people's identity.)

In 1958 the courts took us from our parents and we were split up. My two sisters went to an industrial school in Wexford and me and my three brothers went to Rathdrum. My eldest brother Pete was six, I was four, Paul was two and my youngest brother Anthony was three months. Our parents were alcoholics and had been neglecting us and not feeding us. When we went to Rathdrum, I tell you I have good memories of getting fed three times a day. I remember having breakfasts of cocoa and bread or porridge, it was great. My first five years there were brilliant. The staff were fantastic.

I always remember this nun, her name was Doloreese, Sister Doloreese. That wasn't her proper name, because kids get names mixed up, but to me it will be Doloreese for the rest of my life. This nun she was brilliant. She was beautiful, the picture of loveliness in manner and in looks. I remember we had a going-away party for her when she was leaving. An awful fear hit the place because she was going away. I'll never forget that fear because it was actually the first time I'd ever experienced fear. We knew what was coming because she had said to us "listen life is not going to be like this now when I leave." I was nine at the time

I remember nothing of my life before Rathdrum. It's as if those first four years don't even exist. But my five years with Doloreese are just happy memories. One of the lay staff used to bring us to her uncle's farm and I remember going into a field of turnips and picking a turnip, cleaning it off with our hands and just eating it. We used to eat the centres of the cabbages and leave the leaves. She knew but she didn't mind. She was strict but never too strict to hurt you.

Things changed rapidly after Doloreese left and we got that crazy woman Xavier. We called her Sister "Severia", nobody called her Sister Xavier. Severe was her name and severe was her nature. I remember she kept me up one night, I was the eldest in the place at the time, and I had to scrub the hallway. I can't remember why but I'd probably asked her for something. She never gave anything willingly.

She gave me this scar here with her cross.

He points to the thin white line of a scar on the back of his head.

They used to have these steel crosses hanging from their Rosary beads. I don't remember what I'd done. I was probably in the wrong place at the wrong time.

When Sister Xavier came she brought girls from Goldenbridge with her to work in our place. These girls were orphans and they worked for peanuts. Some of the people she brought with her were bad bitches. She sacked all the lay staff. When she came the standard of food rose but the beatings became more severe.

I know there was school and classes, but I just can't remember going to school. The nuns weren't qualified teachers but they were the ones who taught us. They were only teaching us what they knew, not the curriculum that was set down by the government. What an awful lot of people don't realise is that in the orphanages most of the nuns were the poorer ones. The wealthier ones like Sister Xavier had positions of authority. It was all tied in with the dowry they brought to the convent. One of the poorer ones was Sister Frances, a beautiful woman, and she worked in the scullery and kitchen.

I do have one memory of being in the classroom and the reason I remember it is because this ex-Rathdrum boy came back. He was a priest and I pulled a prank on him. I pulled the chair from under him "sit down there, Father" and as he was sitting down I pulled the chair and he fell on his arse and the whole place cracked up. He took it well but Xavier beat the crap out of me for it. It was a joke, but it was a joke that backfired.

One of the biggest tragedies in Rathdrum was having

to go into the toilet with the little children and having to put their prostate gland back. They'd be left on the pots until they did a motion or urinated. They stayed there until they did. They were about three or four years old. We were eight or nine and we'd be sent down to see if they were okay. The poor kids would be there and they'd be pushing and pushing and there's nothing in their bowels to move. They'd be so long on the pot that there'd be a vacuum created in the pot and it would be stuck to them. Then you'd get the pot off and you'd see the red prostate gland sticking out. It was like a red balloon coming out of their anal passage. You had to get water and push it back in, no toilet paper. It was crazy. It hurt the little kids like hell.

There were all boys in Rathdrum until Sister Xavier came. We used to have to change the babies' nappies. I remember that's how I always used to look after my younger brothers, Anthony and Paul. There was an infants' room and the babies were all in their cots. They weren't taken out or cuddled at all. They were just left, fed and changed, mostly the older kids changed the babies. You weren't allowed to pick them up. I didn't even try to pick Anthony up, because when you're that age you don't know the significance of it. I hadn't even an urge to pick him up because to be affectionate you have to be given affection. What baby see, baby do. Some of the lay staff would give you an old hug now and again. I remember snuggling into this red-headed girl that was there and sitting on her lap and getting a hug off her. That was incredible.

Sometimes they'd send you out to a family for a week-end. You'd be all dolled up like Little Lord Fauntelroy. They used to call them foster parents. I stayed with two sisters in Ashford. They were brilliant and they had the post office. A few years ago I went down to them to see if they were still alive and to say thanks. They really looked after me, they were really nice people. I remember rummaging in the post office and they had all these toys. But I never took a thing, never, because that was the biggest sin. If you took something that meant they would have reported you and you'd never have gone back again.

I used to sleep there overnight and I was mothered and mothered by these two spinster ladies. They were beautiful women. I think even if they didn't give you a penny or they didn't feed you – most of all it was the hug, and putting their arms around you. They gave you affection and it was a really a strange thing because you didn't know what this thing was.

One morning in Rathdrum I woke up and my eldest brother was gone. Just gone. I asked where he was and I was told he was in Artane. They never gave you any warning. About two years later Sister Martin came up to the dormitory and was calling my name. It was just after Easter Sunday, I'll never forget it because I still had two Easter eggs. I was hiding under the bed and I didn't come out because I was all covered in dust and she'd have clipped my ear.

When she left I cleaned myself off and went down to the kitchen and she said "go up and have a bath and there are fresh clothes there for you." This was during the week and I couldn't understand it because only on Sundays did you wear your best clothes.

So up I go and I have my bath and changed. I was given two toys – a truck and a tank, – my two Easter eggs and a little brown case with a change of underwear and a toothbrush. I wasn't allowed to say goodbye to my brothers or anything. I was told I was going to Artane. I was just put on a bus on my own and sent off to Busaras. I was told I'd be met there. It was just after my tenth birthday. That was the age boys were sent on from Rathdrum.

My last year in Rathdrum had been a nightmare so I thought I was escaping, getting out of Hell's Kitchen. But I was going to Alcatraz.

I got up to Busaras dressed in my best clothes and I was met by Brother Joseph O'Connor. He was driving a white van and he said "you'll be one of my boys, because your brother is one of my boys." That meant that I'd be in the Artane Boys' Band, but I didn't know that at the time.

I'll never forget the fear driving up that main avenue at Artane.

He stops and sucks in his breath.

The enormity of the place. It was huge. I'd left this little convent which I thought was massive and then I saw this monolith. It was incredible, a huge complex of buildings. He drove me around to the back door and told me to go upstairs to the dormitory. I met my brother Pete in the hallway. It was two years since I'd seen him but I knew him instantly.

We said nothing, there was just eye contact. I gave him one of my Easter eggs. Then I was sent down to Brother Charles and all the clothes I had on me, the case and the toys were taken off me. Brother Charles gave me my first issue – bull's wool trousers, I'll never forget them. I also got a nightshirt, which I'd never seen in my life before. In Rathdrum we'd worn cotton pyjamas with little bears and things on them.

In Artane it was total fear from the word go. The amount of boys was incredible, about six hundred ranging in ages from ten to sixteen. The majority of the boys there were orphans. But that's really a misnomer because they weren't orphans. You're an orphan if you've no parents, but most of these boys were taken off their parents. If you came from Rathdrum you were a member of the Rathdrum gang straight away, a "Rat" because you came from Rathdrum. If you came from the orphanage in Kilkenny then you were a "Cat" – "Kilkenny cats".

After getting the clothes I was shown my bed. Needless to say I didn't sleep that night. I cried and anybody who tells you that they didn't is talking through his head. Every kid cried.

The next morning we went to Mass. In Rathdrum I used to be able to sing the Mass completely in Latin. I used to love it. The very first day in Artane I went to Mass before breakfast and it was in Irish and I hadn't got a clue. I'd be just mouthing off listening to the other fellows. You were never taught it, you were just supposed to pick it up.

Although there was a congregation there, religion was a very private thing. It was up to you whether you prayed to God or not. It was an instinctive thing, whether you meant what you were saying or not. So if you didn't understand what you were saying how the hell could you mean it? So they took away this privilege that you had of talking to God whether it be in Latin or English. I hadn't a clue of the Irish. I didn't understand what the Latin meant either, but it sounded great and so I knew He understood it.

After Mass there was breakfast – dripping and bread and there was porridge and real strong tea. I was lucky because I was at Pete's table. There was only one Outsider at our table. I probably should explain Outsider. There were two categories in Artane, Outsiders and Convenors. Outsiders were in for truancy and minor theft and they were sent to Artane by the court for anything up to six years. All the outsiders had mums and dads at home. They were from corporation flats, mainly in the city centre. Convenors were all the boys from the convents. Most of the Artane Boys' Band and the choir were Convenors and so was the football team. There were a few Outsiders but not many.

That first morning I went down to get a haircut and your man pinched me with the hair clippers. I said "ow, you're after hurting me" and he hit me a dig.

He wallops one of his hands off the other.

That was my very first lesson – don't open your mouth or you'll get a slap on the puss. I remember I didn't speak to Pete for two days until after I arrived and when I did he told me "keep your head down, your mouth shut and don't look them in the eye."

That's all he said. In Artane you became a collective, you became a part of something really stronger than yourself. You had six hundred brothers there, friends of yours. Convenors were really close together, really close.

I went into my first class and I hadn't a clue what a classroom looked like. You've got to remember that I was a really happy-go-lucky kid with plenty of spunk. "Let's Twist Again" was my party piece in Rathdrum. When I went into the class the Brother said "well what can you do?" and I said "well, I can sing 'Let's Twist Again'." So I did and he said "well I've only one rule in this class, your hands will be shown at all times". In other words if your hands were below the desk you got a slap. Or if your hands were in your pockets that was a bigger sin with him because he thought you were fiddling with yourself. I mean what ten-year-old doesn't?

On this first day I was standing in the yard and Brother Joseph said "you're not supposed to be here, you're supposed to be up with the band." I hadn't a clue where the band was so he brought me up.

It was a different world.

His voice sinks to a whisper.

It was like as if you were in a concentration camp, God forbid, and then you were brought into the officers' quarters of the SS. It was that extreme, it was a completely different world.

The band hall was huge and surrounded by lockers. It would have fitted an entire orchestra and an audience. They didn't even know if I could play a musical instrument but Brother Joe had this thing that if your brother was good at something then you were and Pete was very good at music. To me it was a great adventure – drums, yeah, let me try that! They had a very archaic way of teaching music. If one fellow could play the scale of C then he taught me that. Then when I'd learned everything that he knew and he couldn't teach me any more I went on the next fellow and so on.

You see if you were in the band you got at least two Sundays out every month. You must understand how different the lifestyle was if you were in the band. If you were in the band very few Brothers hit on you, because you were Brother Joe's boys. He selected you and he was very selective. I'd say there were over sixty in the band. The majority of the band members were Convenors, the same with the choir.

You didn't get into the main band for two years. It was a total conveyor system. Brother Joe just picked you. He knew that the boys from the convents were used to singing at Mass. If you turned out not to be musical he let you go. He only took the cream, and I mean the cream.

At one stage a third or more of all the musicians in the Army School of Music were from Artane. There was good pedigree there and there was good musicianship, but the teaching technique was wrong. They taught you how to play an instrument, not what you were playing or the theory. You just played dots and you didn't know anything about chord structure or melody or harmony. But it was freedom! Being in the band was freedom, because you weren't in the workshops or down in the farm. If you were in the band you practised three or four times a day.

Those in the band also had a locker and in it you had four uniforms, maybe eight shirts and four pairs of shoes, as well as your caps and capes. If you had something precious you could put it in there, but if you weren't in the band you had no place to hide stuff. Outside of the band we had nothing of our own, no locker or anything. The whole thing was communal. There were about a hundred and twenty boys to a dorm. The beds were in rows, your head would be almost on the next fellow's feet. We put our clothes in a huge press the size of a house. If you got anything, you'd put it in your bed, that was all. You had nothing that was yours unless you were in the band.

Artane was incredibly self-sufficient. They used to make their own clothes and shoes. They had their own farm and cows for milking, it was massive. It used to take four days for the whole school to pick the potatoes. That's nearly six hundred kids in the fields doing it by hand. That was a great feast, especially when we were burning off the potato stalks, we'd roast the potatoes. They'd be black coming out and we'd pop them open – they were just beautiful. But if you were caught you got walloped. That was the risk you ran.

We used to have to sing the Angelus and say the rosary in the church every day at six o'clock and this is how I came to the eye of Brother P. I was about twelve and a half at this stage and so I was fairly tuned into the place, but three of us were messing in the toilets when we should have been in the church saying the rosary. We tried sneaking into the church but Brother P was on the door and he said "report to me at nine o'clock."

At nine o'clock the three of us were standing outside his room. I'll never forget the fear. We used to call him "Jawbone" because when he was angry his jawbone stood out. I think that's the first time he even noticed I even existed. He looked at me and I forgot Pete's warning "don't look them in the eye. Drop your eyes." I looked him straight in the eye. He asked us what we were doing.

You see there was an unwritten code in Artane that you never focused your eyes on another boy's private parts. You were ashamed of your physical self. It was incredible, the fear that they put into you that the sexual organ was a bad thing. So you never looked down. I remember the first time I saw pubic hair I nearly fainted. I couldn't believe it. I went to Pete and said "hey, your man has got a bush." I hadn't got a clue.

But that night in the toilets we'd been only acting the mick and throwing water, but Brother P thought we were doing something sexual. He turned it around and he turned it into a dirty thing. We all got a whack off him but I tell you I knew I was in for it. I had this sort of sense of foreboding and I thought "oho, I'm in trouble here, kid."

I think it was about two or three months later, because I wasn't thirteen yet, that Brother P woke me up in the middle of the night and said "follow me".

He pauses and lights another cigarette.

An awful lot of people mightn't understand this but when you got a tap and someone said "come here", you went. No matter what time of the day or night it was and you didn't ask why. So when Brother P tapped me I got up out of the bed, groggy and full of sleep. He said "come here, follow me." He didn't look at me and I followed him up the stairs and all I could see was his back. He was still in his full habit.

He stops and can't speak. His eyes fill with tears, the cigarette burns idly between his fingers. He whispers "oh God" before he can continue.

He brought me up to his room and he said "face the door" and then he just raped me. That's it. It was pain, it was pain.

It didn't last more than two minutes. I'd say he was sexually aroused prior to the act. It was very, very painful but I thought it was the norm. I thought every kid got this. I thought it was like another form of punishment. He fucked me out of that room, that's what he did and said "get back down to your bed." I was weak, I was bow-legged. I remember there was blood on my night-shirt.

His eyes fill up again. He takes a mouthful of coffee.

Soon after I realised then that what Brother P did to me was different from the usual punishment because he didn't hit me. He didn't beat the crap out of me and then do it. He just said "face the door and bend down" and then he upped my night shirt and that was it. It was just an animalistic thing. It didn't make sense.

Having been brought up by the nuns and knowing the power of confession I knew the best person you could talk to was the priest. So I went to confession two days later. I was very bad for those two days. I was bleeding from the anal passage. I remember being very withdrawn and not even playing my musical instrument. I just sat there. I didn't care whether I played or not and I used to love it.

I remember Brother Joe asking me was I okay and I walked by him, which was a thing you never did to Brother Joe. But I knew what happened to me was wrong. This is where the majority of people that were abused turn it in on themselves. They blame themselves. I knew that in my heart that I had to go to confession. There was something wrong.

This wasn't a normal beating.

So two days later I went to the priest. I can even remember his aftershave and how he looked but I can't remember his name. I went into the confession box and said that the Brother did something to me and I didn't know why. He said "wait behind". So I waited behind. When he'd finished he brought me over to his room in the Brothers' house and . . .

He pauses again.

. . . then he did exactly the same thing to me. He said "is this what he did to you?" It was just as bad. He left me outside his door. I came out of this room crying and that's when I met Brother Joe walking down the hall. I never told him what happened, I didn't have to say a word. He put his arm around me and gave me an apple and he said "it will never happen to you again." And it didn't.

I gave up living then. Brother Joe protected me but I gave up. I was in and out of the infirmary for two to three years. I got a chronic gland infection and I was brought to specialists who couldn't understand it. I know now it can be psychosomatic.

A few weeks after the rape I got the worst beating I ever got in my life and it was off Brother S. To this day I don't know why. There was another fellow called Brother C, Aero was his nickname. He had very bad "St Andrew's Collar", boils and blisters on his neck, and if you looked at it really quick it looked like an Aero bar. I think the beating had something to do with him. I think he complained to Brother S about me in band practice.

Anyway, Brother S beat me in front of the whole dorm. They were all stood to attention for this. He beat seven colours of crap out of me. He laid into me with the leather and his fists. Pete, my brother, was standing there crying because he couldn't do anything. This man beat me black and blue. He left me for dead. He actually beat me so much that he beat the nightshirt off me. I was left in the foetal position, just totally gone. There were kids in the room crying looking at me.

After the beating I crawled back to the bed and some kid came over and handed me my nightshirt. I was full of shame. It wasn't as bad as Brother P and the priest thing but it wasn't far off it.

What's worse is what he did to me later that night. He came down to me and he said "you can be Annie Oakley in the school play" and he gave me a set of guns. This was less than two hours after the beating. There were welts all over me and my jaw was sore.

About nine weeks after this there was an epidemic of influenza in Artane. They believed in looking after their own. There were no outside people brought in. The epidemic broke out on a Wednesday and the Brothers organised a really special dinner that day. There were chips and Spam and jelly and ice cream for dinner. And if you were in bed you didn't get it. This was a special treat, they were trying to get fellows out of bed. I was feeling very bad but I got up out of the bed and went over to the refectory. I sat down to this smashing meal. Pete looked at me and he said "Jesus, Pat, you don't look good." You could whisper at the table but you couldn't talk. And I whispered "yeah but I'm eating this!". When we finished I got up and went out and collapsed. I remember vomiting everything up.

They got me back up to the room. And this is the enigma of Brother S, the man who'd beaten me black and blue, he stayed by my bed for four nights on the trot. He took incredible care of me. He washed me and bathed me. He had a bottle of tonic water on a chair beside me and he changed my sheets once a day, which was unheard of in Artane. He nursed me really well but he was losing. I was getting worse. I had no will to live. I ended up getting pneumonia with pleurisy. Brother S gave up then and they sent for an ambulance. Of all the kids that got ill in Artane I was the only one taken to hospital.

They gave me a complete examination in the hospital and they had to put a suppository up me to make my bowels work. I had phlegm that you could walk on it was so green. But Brother S came to visit me and every time he came up he'd bring Pete. Then he'd give Pete a day out at the cinema and stuff like that.

I went to Temple Street Hospital and after I started to recover the hospital wouldn't send me back to Artane. They sent me to a nursing home. It was very unusual to go from Temple Street to a nursing home, so maybe they suspected something. The nursing home and hospital were brilliant. It was great to feel protected. I was in the nursing home for at least four weeks. Altogether I think I was out of Artane for about three months because when I went back my hair was shoulder length, I had been gone so long. I buried the memory of the abuse in the hospital. No memory of it. That was it – gone.

Brother Joe collected me from the nursing home and he said "I want to see you later on." To show you how much I didn't care I didn't go up to see him. He asked me did I want to go to the infirmary and I said no. Brother F was in charge of the infirmary and he was a total religious nut. He didn't feed you unless you knew the whole sorrowful mysteries or did novenas. You had to learn a prayer to get fed.

So I went back up to my old bed and then this fellow called Brother McKenna arrived and he said "I'll be looking after you from now on." I have to admit that McKenna was the nicest Brother in Artane. A beautiful man, a real, real gentleman. Brother S never ever hit me again. In fact, very few of them ever hit me after that. I think they had got a fright and it was hushed up. They'd nearly had a fatality on their hands. I really do believe that McKenna was brought in to keep an eye on me. I remember he gave me a pair of football boots and a hurley and he said "I want to see you in goal". So I played in goal for years after that. I started to live again when Brother McKenna came into the picture.

I was still in the band. When we went to Croke Park on All-Ireland day we would arrive at about twelve o'clock on the day of an All-Ireland final and wouldn't get out of there until six. All we'd get was one bottle of Coke and a sandwich. We'd have done the minor game and the senior game and the parades at half time.

At fifteen years of age I had to stand up in front of 93,000 people and sing "The Banks of My Own Lovely Lee" solo. Brother Joe only got people to do that who he thought would be able. There was no thrill attached to it. There was fear that you'd muck it up . . .

His voice hardens.

. . . and if you mucked it up you suffered – so you didn't muck it up. But there were no butterflies. You just went out there and sang. If you didn't do it you were letting down the school and the band and more importantly you were letting down Brother Joe.

You can say what you like about him but Brother Joe taught us etiquette and carriage and he taught us style. He gave us showmanship and a hard neck. He gave us an eye to spot an opportunity. He also taught us how to keep our mouths shut. When you went out from Artane Boys' Band to visit a family you didn't say anything about the school, that was sacrosanct.

Brother Joe taught us how to behave in any company and in any situation. I really do have to admit that he gave me the best thing of all, a passport into any community, music. He also had an awful lot of power. The principal of the Christian Brothers didn't have the power that that man had. He put the Brothers on the market. He had the best show piece for the Christian Brothers that they've ever had and it's still going to this day. That man could weave money, he could spin money out of anything.

He had sixty of us in the band but he was the only one allowed hit us. He hit you where it wasn't seen, and when he hit you you really knew you were being hit. Being in the band didn't mean we were untouchable, but if a Brother hit you he didn't do it in the face. I don't know if Brother Joe made that a rule for the other Brothers not to hit us in the face. When Brother Joe hit you he always put your head between his legs, pulled down your trousers and walloped you on the bum or maybe on the scrotum. He was the most violent man I ever met in my life man but also a genius.

He stops to light another cigarette and draws the smoke deep into his lungs.

Every Brother had his own little pets and these little pets were given privileges but you had to perform a task for these privileges – usually anal or oral sex. You'd see a Brother touching a kid, you might see an arm going around. You might see a sweet being passed. Mostly to the same kid.

I was lucky. Some kids were abused in Artane for the whole six years. Dave, a friend of mine was gang-banged for nearly six years. One Brother brought Dave into the bathroom and bounced him off the four walls and when he was unconscious he did it to him. Then he brought him round he said "this will happen to you every time. Now you can have it with the violence or without the violence." Now Dave being smart said "well can I have a cigarette?" They used to come in and pass him from one to the other and that's the truth. For six years Dave used to perform any act they wanted for a cigarette. He was groomed for abuse. When he left Artane he used to go down and visit the kids in Rathdrum and then he abused them.

We boys never talked about the abuse among ourselves. You see if you were a Brother's pet the other kids didn't talk to you. You were his concubine, his rent-boy. The best thing I ever did after Brother P raped me was to say nothing, because if I'd said anything I would have been abused by others. It sounds as if I'm painting all the Brothers as bad as Brother P. But there were beautiful Brothers there too. I feel that all the Brothers knew what was going on but if they opened their mouths they were moved to the backs of beyond.

An awful lot of people can't understand that paedophiles are predators. They can look in a room and pick the child out they know in their heart and soul they can molest and that child won't open their mouth. I think of the five "F's" of the paedophile –

They Find You
They Fool You
They Feel You
They Fuck You
They Forget You

In our band uniforms we were a paedophile's dream. We had a lovely red and navy uniform and we looked like little miniature soldiers. We had several different uniforms including a walking-out uniform. We even had a new one that was actually made in America. We had three pairs of shoes including black and white spats and they had to be polished with Vaseline on the white leather and boot polish on the black.

There was a fire in early January in Artane. Three lads were under the stage having a fag and the band hall and every bit of equipment in it was burned. Brother Joe lost the best music library in Ireland at the time. That was a great day. We watched the whole thing burn. We thought it was brilliant. It was the best day of my life. You might think that I would be sorry that all the band stuff was burned, but it was only a means for Brother Joe to make money. We were all there cheering. We were a good four hundred feet away from it and we could feel the heat. It was brilliant!

Brother Joe had taken the band on tour to the States for two weeks just after the fire. Instruments were donated from everywhere. When we came back there was nobody in Artane. It had closed.

I don't know why it closed, but I think it was getting to the stage where people were starting to ask what was going on in there. Why were so many kids coming out of there totally zipped up? If you take a number of the kids that have been in there, they're homosexual. Don't get me wrong, I don't think that's necessarily a bad thing, but maybe they could have had a proper sexual existence if they didn't go through what they did.

It's bad to know only that aspect of life, to only know that sexual experience, and never to experience the want or the need for a woman. The Brothers changed you into what they were through no fault of yours. That's where I was lucky when Brother Joe said it wouldn't happen to me again and he kept his word.

When I came back the last person I said goodbye to was Brother Charles, the man who took my clothes that very first day. I was the last one to be issued with going-out kit and I issued it to myself. He said "go in there and pick whatever you want." I was the last boy to officially leave Artane in 1969.

Don't get me wrong. I have some good memories of Artane, especially with the band. But we were very, very cheap labour and they made big money out of us. I suppose even now if I heard the band was in trouble I'd probably go up and help them out.

It's an incredible thing, but to this day I'd cross the road if a nun was coming down the same side, or a priest or a brother or anybody in the collar, even if it was a Church of Ireland one. It's a stigma that they've left me with. But in saying that I'm very, very religious now. I pray, I pray to God. He's very much there for me.

Anyway when I left Artane I joined the Army School of Music at fifteen and a half. I was underage but the Brothers got paid for every one of their boys who joined up. The Army was completely different in some ways, because I now got paid £2.3s 4d. to do what I previously used to get hit to do. We could also go out three nights a week and we got three square meals a day. Otherwise it was as if there was no transition, it was like going from one Artane into another.

I ended up as an instructor in the Army School of Music for ten years. Almost three quarters of the staff of the school were from Artane and they all had Brother Joe's techniques. I led a crazy life. I hated authority and was constantly in trouble. I didn't know it, but I had buried something in me. Even though I buried it my behaviour was crying out for attention for somebody to say "what's wrong with you?" But you don't get that in the Army. So I was in the wrong place. I started drinking heavily.

I got married at twenty-one and I don't know how my wife stayed with me. But then she's a saint – she must be to stick with me.

It's like I didn't let people get to know me. I put up this facade and eventually I didn't even like the facade. I was full of a fear that I couldn't let out. I had become a heavy drinker and was out with the lads when I should have been home with the wife. I was Jack the Lad, the life and soul of the party. On the outside it looked like I had so much confidence, I was the big man, but behind it all I had no self-belief. Behind it all there was fear. It was all a facade and I just wanted to cry on somebody's shoulder and say "this is what happened" but I didn't know what happened.

If there was a problem I'd just lash out, I'd get very physical. I was so institutionalised – Rathdrum, Artane, and then twenty-two years in the Army. When I left the Army I went into another institution – a school. I taught PE and music and I was very good at it. But behind it all there was this self-destruct button that I was hitting. The principal once said to me "Pat, if your head was screwed on you'd be out of this world. You're heading for a big bang." He could see it. I was doing my job very well but I had to have certain amount of alcohol on me to be able to do it.

I knew I had to break away from institutions. It was really hard and I had to just stop and say "no that's it." But I was afraid to walk away. Eventually I got myself into a situation where I had to leave the school. Then I went into a tailspin, straight down. I was so far down that I was below the earth. I completely went into myself and became totally introspective. I disregarded my family totally.

When I left teaching it was the very first time in my life, since I was four, that I wasn't being looked after by the government in an institution. Every manner you have is related back to the institutions you were in. You're never yourself. You're living by rules that *they* make. You're so disciplined in the way they've taught you that it is so hard to find yourself.

I was really pissed off being institutionalised and I wanted to be out there where you had to fight. But I didn't realise the enormity of the fight that I had to put in. I was drinking very heavily. I was the first one in the pub at half-ten. It was just to be part of an institution and I picked alcohol as the institution I was going to be part of. I was on uppers and downers and I was obnoxious. I was very, very lucky that I was married to such a good person. Really lucky.

After I left the teaching it took me about a year and a half to go right down. One day I just sat in the pub and cut my wrist. I woke up in James's Hospital. I remember taking another blade out of my pocket in the hospital and a male nurse took it from me. He was a very nice bloke and he said to me "there's a priest in there. Do you want to talk to him?" That's when the memory of the abuse came straight back into my head – bang.

He clicks his fingers.

I said "what the fuck do you think has me in here? I wouldn't talk to a priest if you paid me." When the memory came back it was like a weight off my heart. It was an incredible weight. I was getting back to being my own person not this thing that I'd created.

They brought me upstairs and I think they had me watched. This fellow came around, just an ordinary Joe Soap and he asked me how I was. I said I was grand and he said "you weren't too good when you came in were you?" I said "no, I wasn't, but I found out why." So I told him. He was the first person I ever told. It turned out that he was the priest that the male nurse had told me about. I told him the whole story and he was crying at the bed. He said that what I should do is to tell the whole world. "I can't do anything for you because I'm a priest. I'd be going against the Catholic Church and I can't do that. But tell everybody that you can tell and you scream and you make sure it's heard."

I made a conscious decision to tell my family altogether. When I told my brothers they reacted as if they were all abused as well. They felt every aspect of it. There was silence. My wife and my two children were there.

I've no fears about telling this story any more. I've no apologies to make. I felt it had been my fault and that's why I blocked it out. The victim always turns it in on himself and says "if I wasn't there it wouldn't have happened or I must have done something wrong for that to have happened." But that's all twisted. That's how you rot inside. Couple that with being institutionalised for thirty-five years – it's like you become a different bloke – it's like you become a dual personality. I was fed up being a dual person, being one person to myself and another person to the rest of the world.

After I told my family I asked to be put into a psychiatric ward but the psychiatrist said I didn't need it. I didn't need to be in another institution. So I prayed, but not to Christ or anybody like that. Nothing to do with the Catholic Church, nothing to do with institutionalised religion. I was given a present of a book called *The Autobiography of a Yogi* and I got great strength out of that. I prayed to God just straight, just me and him. No church, no nothing.

I didn't go for counselling or therapy but I talked to people. I eventually worked out for myself that you have to find it in your heart to forgive yourself, especially if there's nothing there to forgive. It wasn't me that did this thing. It had got nothing to do with me.

It helps when you tell everybody, but then you have to get off the euphoric buzz. You can't stay out there crusading all the time. You've got to get on with your life. I remember somebody saying that when the good feeling finished, I'd be left very low. So I knew it was going to come and I knew that if I wasn't prepared it could bring me right back down again.

I told everybody and anybody and then I went back teaching at my own leisure and I really enjoyed it. I wasn't making big money but I was giving something back to kids at my request – not anybody else's. The kids that I had brought me back up again. It was the children that I had so much respect for that brought me back in to myself.

My wife stood by me all the way. For such a small woman she was a great tower of strength. We've a good marriage. Like everybody else's marriage we've had some rough times and some bad times.

For a while I worked in holistics and massage and that taught me an awful lot. Holistics is a thing you learn from yourself first. You have to heal yourself first. If you can see the individual you're working with, leaving out the sex and gender, and see the pain of the individual, there's no way you can abuse that individual. Through me helping people I'd say they helped me more. They gave me more than I gave them. In my own way they were giving me therapy. They were letting me back into the world of touch for the first time maybe since I was four. They were allowing me to help them and they were really helping me. For every person

I've ever rubbed I've always said a prayer, before and after, one of help and one of thanks.

A year ago we decided to move to the West. You can't change your memories but you can block them out and I feel that's the most dangerous thing you can do. I was only prepared to move if my wife wanted to. I owed her the chance to find herself because she spent twenty-two years looking after me and the two kids.

She picked where we would move to and I'm so happy she picked where she did, because we probably fell into the best community you could ever fall into. I still do the occasional massage. I train the football team and I teach music. It's changed my wife so much, she's out walking and she's starting to lose weight and she's getting her hair done. She is starting to live and if I can make a good life for her then I know I've repaid the debt of twenty-two years.

What did the abuse take from me? It took *me*. It took away *me*.

It took the happy-go-lucky kid and put him in a corner for twenty-seven years. I left that *me* in the corner and I went around as another person. But you see I was double jeopardied – when I went to the confessor to tell him what the Brother had done, instead of getting solace and comfort I got exactly the same thing as I did from the abuser. So therefore it blew my religion out the window and it blew my faith in telling people. So therefore I didn't tell. So when I told everybody I felt I was cleansed. But I made a mistake – I had nothing to be cleansed for. That took time to realise as well. I was trying to clean myself but I wasn't dirty and that's the sin of the abuser. He leaves you in such a mental state that you feel completely dirty.

I think cutting my wrist was the opening of a door. Now, I'm not saying it was a good thing to do – it was a crazy thing to do. But the only way I had of releasing my pain was to inflict pain on me, so that I could get rid of the pain that was inflicted on me. It was the start of me being the kid again that I'd been at four years of age.

Now I don't feel dirty and I don't care what people think about me telling the story. I know I did nothing. I was just there and that's all. I didn't break any trusts. He broke every trust that was placed on him by the Catholic Church and the authorities. He broke all trust and turned me into something that I wasn't.

I'm still confused about certain things, but I'm a much nicer person to me and I'm a much nicer person to my wife and children. I can still fly off the handle like anybody but there's no violence. There's not this really bad violence.

I have great self-belief now and I don't do anything that I don't want to do. There's no guilt now. I was carrying the Brother's guilt and the priest's guilt. I'm as happy as a pig in manure. I've never been as happy as this.

MOLLY

MOLLY

"It would invade my mind at the most intimate of moments. I always felt there were three in the bed."

She is warm, bubbly and charming. She is wearing a long, flowered dress, has black curly hair, and exudes a zest for life. She loves to laugh. Now in her mid-thirties she is married with two young children.

She travels to Dublin and I meet her in the city centre. We drive to my house and settle ourselves in the sitting room.

I had been working abroad for two years when my father died. I was twenty-five at the time and I decided to come back to Ireland and look for a job here in the West. I was out hill-walking one day about six months after he died and when I came into the house my mother said "look who's come to see us." It was Father X, an old family friend who had just returned from Australia. The most immediate sensation I had was of the smell of his aftershave pervading the room. It was as if this huge postcard popped up into my head of things that had happened to me nearly fifteen years before. When I saw him I felt revulsion, my stomach heaved.

Memories came back to me there and then for the first time in fifteen years. I had this gut feeling that something had happened with him. I had an image of him abusing me and of me being aged about ten.

Her voice trembles.

I was into hill-walking at the time and Mammy said "you must bring Father X up the mountains for a walk." I was very curt with her, which was unlike me, and I got away from him as quickly as I could. I could see Mammy thought there was something wrong with me.

I went out that night with pals and when I came home I couldn't sleep. Mammy came in to me. I told her what had happened. It was the first time I had ever put it into words. I think I used the word "abuse", and said that he had sexually abused me as a child. Even though abuse wasn't much talked of in the media at that time I remember I had the words to describe it. She was just horrified. She was emotionally very raw herself because it was just six months after my father had died.

Father X had been living in Australia and this was his first visit to us for years. He had called to express his condolences for my father's death. As well as the revulsion I felt when I saw him there was also this very strong feeling in my head "you never thought I'd grow up and realise that what you did was wrong." I was twenty-five, I was a fully fledged adult. He said nothing to me.

Her eyes fill with tears.

X was staying in our house and the next morning when

I came down Mammy said "he's gone. I said nothing to him but he knew from the way I looked at him that I knew." She didn't actually confront him because she was so weak and emotionally low at the time. I don't think she had the energy to confront him. She was stunned, really.

Mary, a very good friend, had come back to Ireland at the same time as me. She had also been abroad and we both came home around the same time. We lived in each other's pockets. We were in the pubs seven nights a week together, getting back into circulation. I told her about the abuse and she was great.

Molly starts to cry.

I can't really remember exactly what she said but she was great and said things like "oh God you poor thing. The bastard. Fuck him." I can still see the spot in the local park where I told her. I remember thinking "I've dealt with it now because I told somebody." I thought that was it – cured.

We used to walk the legs off ourselves, up and down the mountains and that was very healing for me. At the time I was also dealing with my father's death which had been very sudden. He was only fifty-two when he died. Dealing with the past abuse was almost secondary, and yet it was there hovering.

When I was a child we had a small family business and Father X was a young priest in his late twenties taking a sabbatical from the priesthood. He helped out generally around the place and he'd play the piano at night. Our family were great for taking in lame ducks and he became like part of the family. He was treated like our older brother or like a favourite cousin who was going through a rough patch.

My parents thought that he was great and that he needed to be minded. Although he was an employee he was more like a family friend. So he ate with us and was around us a lot. If we were going to bed he would read us our bedtime story.

I know now from profiles of abusers that they worm their way into a family and gain positions of trust. I feel he was always hovering, circling. I think he stayed with us for a year. I have photographs of him with us when I was about seven. He also used to come and work for the summers.

I'm not sure how it started but I have an image of sitting on his lap and him teaching me to play the piano.

She glances across at the piano in the sitting room and immediately looks away.

To this day I'd find it very hard to have a piano in my house. He abused me while he was playing the piano. That's one of my earliest memories – me sitting on his lap and him having an erection and rubbing up against me and fondling my breasts. I knew "God, this isn't quite right", but didn't really know what was happening.

I have another image. These images are like a series of postcards in my head that flick up in turn.

Another picture is of him out in the boat with us on the lake. But that would have been for public viewing – that image would have been perfect. Mammy and Daddy and us kids were in the boat. That would have been harmless, that would have been untainted. But now I see how he was kind of hovering, circling.

Another image is of him in my bedroom touching me, always in silence. Getting me to touch him and to masturbate him. That feeling of revulsion. It was like a silent scream. I used to look back and think "why didn't I tell Mammy and Daddy?" They were great parents. But I looked back at photographs and realised that I was only a child and I didn't know what to do with the feeling of awkwardness. There was that silence, the blanket of silence. I don't remember any words spoken.

Another strong memory is the smell of aftershave mingled with the smell of sperm. He used to finger around and inside my vagina. Digital rape they call it now. There was never penetration with his penis, I don't remember it, anyway.

I began to menstruate on my twelfth birthday. This was around the time the abuse stopped. I made my Confirmation a few months later. So my earliest puberty would have been mixed up with that feeling of abuse and silence and a feeling that I didn't have any power over the situation.

I saw a photograph of me making my Confirmation and it was interesting to see that I had long, straight hair, parted in the middle, and it almost completely covered my face. I don't know how I didn't break my neck because it was like a curtain of hair over my face.

I was chronically shy during those years. My mother says that she was worried about my shyness. I couldn't cope with even minor situations. I remember I didn't think much of myself at that time. I thought of myself as inadequate. There was one relative who, whenever she met me, would look me over from top to toe and I never felt I quite measured up. I somehow didn't make the mark. I was unworthy.

My parents never suspected anything and that was part of my anger towards my father. But by the time I remembered the abuse he was dead so I couldn't actually be angry at him personally. I was also angry at my mother. Where were they? How was it able to happen?

My mother and I haven't talked about it a whole lot. I felt that because Daddy wasn't around for her that I couldn't be angry towards her, even though I was for awhile. She did say to me "and you know X told us his sabbatical was like an enforced sabbatical." I realised then, as she realised, that he had been suspended because of reading certain material – probably of a dubious sexual nature. But the way he had told it when we were kids was "aren't they so narrow-minded in the seminary."

After I remembered the abuse I had a wild year or two. I had been very religious before that when I was abroad. So although I was still a Christian I was kind of a wild Christian. I was always off to the pub or the folk club. I enjoyed the wilder side of things and still do.

So when I came home I went completely wild. We were out every night. Every week-end we were climbing mountains and every night we were climbing bar stools. It was just being young and wild and having a bit of money. I had got a teaching job by then.

I remember one night when I went to the pictures with my friend Mary and another friend who I'd told about the abuse – there was a film *Mona Lisa* with Bob Hoskins in it. And all of a sudden there was a guy abusing his niece in the movie. It was quite obvious he was abusing her in that murky, knot-in-your-gut, kind of way. I remember the three of us looked at each other, and this is how good they were for me, without saying a word the three of us just stood up and walked out. They were great.

I was also quite promiscuous at that tine. Looking back I'd say it was almost vengeful on men. I was quite – I hate the expression – a mickey-teaser really. I would say there was an element of revenge. I would never have complete intercourse with them. It was as if I had power. I would lead fellows on to a certain stage and then disappoint them. Of course a lot of it was fear of my mother and getting pregnant as well.

She laughs.

A lot of my friends were getting married and I found that hard. I remember one year I went to ten weddings on my own. I was always invited to bring a friend and I'd reply that I'd love to come but I'd be on my own. There was this feeling of being left on the shelf. I was about twenty-six at this stage.

I was great pals with a fellow called Anthony all through this. He worked in a hotel and he was always very nice to me, but because he was nice I had no time for him. I was always going for the bastards. The kind that would never commit themselves. Looking back on it I see I wasn't ready for a commitment, but at the same time I craved it.

There was one guy that I had a big fling with on holidays in the west in August. He was from Dublin. When I went back to West Clare at Halloween to see him he arrived with his girlfriend of three years. That was the kind of guy I went for and I'd be grateful for any few crumbs they threw me. I'd be thrilled if they just left to go home with me, but I never felt I could make any demands of them or be worthy enough to have a relationship. I would be okay to go home with and have a shift, as they would call it in Kerry, but not be called a girlfriend. I didn't really a have steady boyfriend during that time.

I had known Anthony for ages and he used to ask me out to things. I would make up some excuse not to go. I kept hoping that one of the other shitty guys would invite me out. Then Anthony invited me to a New Year's Eve Dance, it was the thing to get invited to. But I made an excuse not to go. I assumed the other guy would invite me to something – and of course he didn't. He went off with another girlfriend and I ended up watching telly with my mother. I thought it served me right.

Two weeks after Halloween I met Anthony again at a fancy dress party. He offered to buy me a drink and I refused. I was playing it very cool hoping this other guy, one of the shits, would come. My sister said "if I were you I wouldn't be so cool to Anthony, I heard two women talking about him in the loo." Of course forbidden fruits are sweet, so I said "do you know, I think I will have that drink after all."

She laughs again.

I had treated him like dirt up to this point. Because he was so nice I used to just walk over him.

We ended up together that night. After all my messing around with different fellows it just felt so right with him. As the physical side of our relationship was developing I had an awful lot of flashbacks to the abuse. So I told Anthony about the guy who had abused me because I realised it was beginning to affect our relationship. That was the first time I was aware that what had happened fifteen years before was affecting me now. When I told Anthony he was great about it and I remember thinking "yes, he's special if I can say this to him." He was very angry with the abuser and wanted to go and kill him.

The other thing was that he was very gentle with me. He's a very gentle man. He was so understanding about the physical side of our relationship and never put me under pressure. That was very important and we took things very slowly. Despite this it was never great for me or for him. We never spoke much about the abuse. I felt that it was my fault and that I should be able to put the abuse out of my head. Push it aside and it will go away. But it would invade my mind at the most intimate of moments. I always felt there were three in the bed.

We got married a year after we started going out with each other. We had had a lovely courtship and the wedding was great. Physically it was okay but the memories were always there. I suppose I faked things a lot because I wanted Anthony to feel good and I wanted to feel good myself. I thought if I told myself it didn't matter often enough then I'd believe it myself.

We come home from out honeymoon and I was pregnant. We were delighted. All I'd ever wanted was to be married and to have babies, loads of them. Anthony was thrilled. He felt so honoured and proud at the thought of being a father. I loved being pregnant. I loved that kind of smug feeling. Mike was born in

August by Caesarean section. Having the section made me feel powerless. It was a real slap in the face because I thought I would give birth so naturally that I could go out and have babies in the fields. It didn't happen. I was a bit blue after the baby was born. At first I was elated and then I went down. But I got over it and shook it off fairly quickly.

We were very badly organised when it came to money and didn't budget properly. We went into things without thinking them through. When Mike was a year old we moved to a new house.

To the outsider I'd say we would have been quite a happy couple. Looking back I don't think I lived with the abuse thing very much at that time because there were so many other major issues to be dealing with – such as surviving, basic house-keeping, learning to be a mother, learning to be a wife and working outside the home. So it was just a time of survival. There wasn't much time or energy to deal with other things.

Then we decided we'd love another baby and so we planned Joe. We never seemed to have done much planning before. He was planned to arrive in November which would be a quiet time for us. I knew I was going to have another Caesarean section. The great thing about having a section was that I knew exactly when it would be. I was so proud of how organised we were.

When I had our first baby by section I had an epidural and I was a bit freaked out at being wide awake when they cut me open. I'm very squeamish and can't even watch injections in television hospital dramas. With the second birth all my instincts told me to have a general anaesthetic. But I disregarded my own feelings completely and went along with Anthony who wanted to be present at the birth. He couldn't be there if it was a general anaesthetic and the gynaecologist said that it would be better for the baby if I had an epidural. Looking back now I realise that I surrendered my control there. It was my body, my choice, but I gave them the power over me. Doing that was wrong for me, but hindsight is a great thing.

I was wheeled down for the section and when the doctor cut me he nicked a vein and the blood literally nearly hit the wall. I was as awake as I am now for all of this. I could see them looking at each other and it was as if they had those speech bubbles that you see in comics coming out of their mouths saying " oh shit!" Nobody was talking to me because they were all focused on my stomach. I started to get sick into the mask and as I was throwing up I kept thinking "it wasn't supposed to be like this!" I desperately wanted someone to talk to me. It was the silence that reminded me of the abuse. I wasn't aware of it then but it did bring back that memory of powerlessness.

She hesitates for some moments at the recollection.

I can still feel that sense of powerlessness sometimes over relatively insignificant things. Family events can overwhelm me. We had Mike's Communion recently and I would feel intimidated by some of our relatives. Because I sometimes think they're looking down on me. But his Communion was like a coming of age for me as well. Some of these relatives would be heavy drinkers and into spirits and everything. And I just said to myself "no, this is our house and we're just sticking to beer and wine." That was a huge thing for me – to make a stand.

After Joe's birth I needed a blood transfusion. There had been recent scandals about contaminated blood and I freaked out inside myself when I saw the bag of blood going up and going into my arm. But outwardly I started cracking jokes. That's the way I survived. The nurse would say "are you all right there now?" and I'd say "well, you could slip a gin and tonic into the bag." Whereas inside I'd be saying "Jesus Christ!". For a couple of years after the birth I often felt so miserable that I was actually convinced that I had Hepatitis C.

When Joe was two days old the paediatrician came in to talk to me and he told me that the baby had a heart murmur. I was devastated. Then the gynaecologist came in and said "Molly, you have post natal-depression." He had spotted it because I was in hospital longer than usual because of the section. I'm eternally grateful to him for that because I was a mess.

The tears started flowing on day two and they just kept flowing. Breastfeeding failed for me on day four when the milk came in. It literally couldn't come out. I remember this nurse with an electric breast pump and nothing coming out of my breasts but the tears were flowing out of my eyes. I felt "I can't even do this, the most basic of womanly acts." I felt a total failure.

She cries. Her tears spill over and for awhile we stop.

The gynaecologist felt that I could do with a bit of help to cope with the post-natal depression and he put me on anti-depressants for six weeks. He said that the depression was caused by a chemical imbalance. That helped me a little bit. But I still felt such a failure because none of the rest of my friends had had it. I found it very hard to come to terms with the fact that I was on medication for depression. The gynaecologist said that the medication wouldn't knock me out but would just take the edge off the pain. To the outward eye I was strong and well able to cope but the reality was so different. I couldn't even deal with visitors in the hospital.

She continues to cry as we talk, squeezing the words out between her tears.

When I got home I was just about able to cope. I had Mike to cope with as well, he was just a toddler and in the throes of tonsillitis. Joe was an extremely good baby but even that worried me. I thought he was so good because he was too weak to cry. "He's so sick because of his heart that he can't even cry." At six weeks I had to come off the anti-depressants and I just wondered how I was going to get through this. I felt my life was a disaster.

I couldn't even cope with small things. I'd no appetite. I lost a pile of weight and everybody complimented me. It was almost funny that people had this idea that it was so good to be thin no matter what was happening inside you. I did look great but I felt awful. I was just drinking coffee and eating nothing.

I was full of anger, anger at Anthony. He would come home and I'd say "did you have lunch out today?" and if he said that he had and that it was nice I'd think "huh, well for you". If he said it wasn't nice, I'd think "well tough, at least you're getting it served up to you in the company of adults and I'm here at home on my own." I was very angry and he could not do anything right. When he came in I'd either burst out crying or eat the head off him. "Tetchy" was the word he used to describe me. That lasted for about a year and a half.

All through this he was trying to be a back-up, taking over the lads when he'd come home. He did all the night feeds and he was great. But he was a bit scared because I wasn't myself. I was very quietly, silently miserable. I also had awful back pain from an old whiplash injury that seemed to really flare up and I had terrible headaches.

In the evenings when I was getting the tea just before Anthony came home the boys would usually be quiet. At that quiet time the shadow of the abuse would pass over me. I've very strong memories of standing at the cooker and stirring a pot and of this shadow passing over my shoulder. With it there would be a flashback to the abuse mixed with a flashback of Joe's birth and the blood and everything. They were kind of superimposed on each other and I would nearly get sick with the enormity of it.

So then I thought it was the birth that was causing all these problems. So I chatted it out with Anthony about how awful I had felt at the birth. When I told him I thought "right, I've said it now, I've it dealt with now." That's what I had felt about the abuse as well. I thought that the telling of it was dealing with it – which of course it wasn't.

Even though Anthony couldn't say or do anything right, I still needed him so much. I was clinging to him like you'd cling to a rock. So if he had to go to a function at work or a match I was like a lunatic. I was like a bitch for a week beforehand and a week after. I expected him to be there, literally like a lap dog, for every minute of every day and night that he wasn't working. Even though I was horrible to him when he was there.

I was going to acupuncturists, bio-energists, alternative homeopathic doctors, physiotherapists. I spent a fortune on these different things. I was also teaching and running a small business. The money seemed to be coming in but it was going out as fast. Life was very complicated and I couldn't see any way out.

During this year and a half of misery I felt so low that I thought of suicide two or three times. I used to look at the boys and think "they'd be better off without me."

Tears roll down her cheeks.

I found the smallest things so hard to deal with. My strongest feeling was "how can I mind them if Mammy and Daddy couldn't mind me?" As well as the trauma of Joe's birth reminding me of the abuse there was also the fact that I was now the mother of two children. I used to nearly pass out with the fear that I wouldn't be able to protect them. I was almost allergic to them and I just wasn't able to enjoy them at all. I fed them and I changed them but I was petrified.

I was completely unable to cope. I was going through the motions from one day to the next. "Powerless", again the word comes back. I felt powerless even in terms of my own life and the way I wanted to run my life. I was on a treadmill and I was going nowhere. Then I thought Anthony would definitely be better off without me, because he was just trying to do his best and I was being an awful bitch.

He'd come in and I'd either burst out crying or I'd eat the head off him. At this stage other people would have thought I was well over the blues. "You're great now and you're in great form. You're thin and you look great." But I was awful. I had two faces – one for the public and Anthony got the real one where the mask came off.

So one day he came in and said "if you like I'll organise some help for you." I thought he meant more help with the children but he said "I mean psychiatric help." So that really shook me and I kind of straightened myself for a while after that. I said "oh Jesus, I'd better really cop on to myself." It was as if I was being a bold child or being petty.

It worked for a couple of weeks all right but then I was just too miserable. I was desperately unhappy and the shadow over my shoulder was there nearly all the time now. Anthony didn't know about the shadow because I thought that by telling him about the abuse before we were married I had dealt with it. We hadn't really talked about it since our wedding except one time when I was expecting our first baby and Anthony was using a particular aftershave. It reminded me of the abuser's aftershave and I asked him to put it in the bin. Anthony found that very hard to take, because he thought it wasn't part of our lives any more. But it was there, lurking like a ghost.

The crunch came one day and I thought "it's our marriage. Our marriage is really just not working out." The next day I said "do you think we should separate?" I said it with all seriousness, from my toes up I meant it. I was convinced, as I had been with the suicide feeling, that the three of them would be better off without me. Anthony just burst out laughing and said "Molly, I'm going to stop *Hello!* magazine coming into this house." So that made me laugh at myself. It was the first time I'd laughed in a long time because all through this I had completely lost my sense of humour.

Shortly after this I was reading *The Sunday Tribune* at the time the Father Brendan Smyth case was getting huge publicity. I saw his face and I would love if they burnt that footage they have of him on the television because it's so menacing. Naturally for me it brought back the feelings of abuse and I nearly felt that I had been abused by him.

Then I just lost it. When I read that article it was as if a cork flew out off a bottle. The torrents of tears and anguish that had been building up in me burst out and I just sobbed and sobbed. I said "Anthony, you've no idea how miserable I've been feeling about it", and I told him all about the flashbacks. He said "I had no idea." It was the very last thing that I thought was the cause of my misery. I was picking on all sorts of other things looking for a reason. But it was finally like the real truth had come.

The newspaper article had mentioned the Rape Crisis Centre as a place to go for help. I never realised that they dealt with abuse, I always thought it was rape. I decided to ring them the next day. When I phoned I had a feeling of relief and of awful sadness, just saying "I've been abused." It was like a bereavement. I couldn't stop crying and I had that sense of shock. I was in torment. I got an appointment for the next day. My counsellor was great and I connected with her. Anthony took the day off work and drove me over – he was that supportive.

At an early stage of my counselling I wanted to tell the whole world what had happened to me. A defiant gesture – this was not my fault, it happened to me! I could understand Sinead O'Connor taking the full page ad in *The Irish Times* telling about her abuse. When I explained this urge to Anthony he jokingly said "oh Jesus Molly not the local paper!" That was one of the few laughs we had at that time.

At the beginning of the counselling I was very raw, it was like a bereavement. I had lost my childhood. This childhood that I thought in my head had been so perfect. It wasn't as it had seemed. I remember writing at the time "Nothing is as it seems." That feeling of the outside face of the abuser being so different to what goes on inside them.

The counselling was just such a relief. I was thirty three-at this stage and the physical reaction from my body was just incredible. It reacted to everything that had been stored up. My back gave way, it was like springs flying everywhere. I was nauseous for about two months. As I began to open up the memory box the picture postcards would come more frequently. It was like letting them flow after twenty years of keeping them at bay. Once they began to flow it was like I couldn't stop them. I cried almost constantly.

I began to get very heavy bleeding, almost to the point of haemorrhaging. This went on for four months. A hysterectomy was even suggested. I told my gynaecologist my story and he was so kind. I remember he put his hand on my arm and said "God love you."

He was so soothing. I took a big risk telling him, but I was glad I did. If I was advising anybody I'd say only tell people to whom it will make a difference in their dealings with you. You don't have to tell the woman at the check-out in Quinnsworth, but your gynaecologist is a very important person.

I remember at this time telling a girl what had happened to me and she just couldn't take it at all. I had to learn that not everybody can deal with hearing about abuse. I've learnt the hard way. There were two people I told who couldn't handle it. If that happens, you're left there with your guts on the floor and somebody just steps over them, it's a very hard feeling. I also told some other friends who were, and still are, great about it. They were very supportive, especially through the beginning of the counselling when I was very low and in need of a car or someone to mind the boys.

My lowest point was when I was reacting to the medication I was on for the bleeding. I was totally lethargic and couldn't handle the kids or even talk to people. I went to the doctor one day and I said "I can't go on like this, I can't cope with anything." I cried all over him. He decided I should try another drug and I asked him to read out the side effects. He said that the side effects included "emotional lability". I'd never heard the word before but he explained that it meant not being unable to handle things. So I said "forget it. I'm not going on any more drugs." This was a huge turning point for me because I wasn't passive in somebody dealing with me or my body. That was a very big thing for me to say because usually I'd say "yes sir, no sir, whatever you say."

So then I got some nutritional advice from a friend who was involved in acupuncture and nutrition and started eating properly and taking vitamins. The haemorrhaging soon stopped and my next period was absolutely normal. It's extraordinary but at the time neither me nor my gynaecologist linked the bleeding and the physical symptoms with the start of the counselling for the abuse.

As well as dealing with the abuse the counselling also taught me how to communicate better with Anthony in particular and to realise that everything is linked. It was hugely important sexually, because the first most important thing I learned was that I wasn't to blame. I had felt guilty, dirty and unworthy and it had seriously affected our love-making. I had very low self-esteem inside even though outside I might have actually looked quite cocky. The counselling also helped me absolve myself of the guilt and it helped me to forgive my mother and father.

My counsellor had suggested that we stop making love for a while. Her explanation was that my first experience of sex was abuse, so that any other experience of it would bring up the abuse thing for me. I had to clear the slate and deal with the abuse. It worked. We didn't make love for maybe two months and it brought back all the cuddling and the loving without intercourse. It was like dating again. I always knew Anthony was special but I never realised of what precious stuff he was made until it came to the crunch.

I remember one Friday him coming home from work and I was just hanging on like an alcoholic waiting for a drink. I just about made it until he came home and then I went down to our room. I experienced such a torrent of crying. It was a big part of the grieving process. Just crying for my lost innocence which I could never have back again. As a child I shouldn't have been sexualised and I was and I find that very sad. I was giving vent to all of that. I was down on our bed just crying, crying, crying. It was real primeval stuff. Anthony came down and just held me and I sobbed and sobbed. It is still one of my most precious memories of our relationship that he was there for me for that. He had the insight to know that I didn't just need him to mind the children but to hug me as well.

Her tears come again.

The counselling has made a huge difference to our marriage. We are now much more open with each other. Before I went for counselling I used to say with pride "God, we never fight", like it was a trophy. We didn't fight, but we weren't really that happy because I was too afraid to fight. I didn't trust myself because I'd all this raging anger, misery and turmoil knotted up inside me. I didn't fight because I think I didn't have confidence in our relationship. If there was something bugging me I didn't feel I had the right to be bugged. I felt he was right and I was wrong.

Now I'm a great fighter. Maybe every six months we'll have a humdinger of a row. It's fantastic and it clears the decks. Now I say with pride "yes, I'm brilliant at fighting, we've great fights." I've the confidence in myself and in our relationship to have a row.

I can honestly say that since I finished counselling two years ago I haven't had a blue day, not even a blue hour. I've had a few down moments but I can acknowledge them now, whereas before the counselling I'd have felt I wasn't entitled to feel low and just bury my feelings.

It used to be the same at work. I had a boss at one stage who was a bastard to everybody. Eleven of the staff left within six months. If there was a conflict I'd feel the guilty one, as if I was somehow at fault. I now have to take a deep breath and say "you are not to feel guilty about this." Other people would say "fuck him, that's his problem." But I could never see that. If somebody was in bad form I always assumed that it was something that I had done. Now I look at them and I say "hangover or marital problems, or whatever. It has nothing to do with me." I used to take on other people's feelings and assume they were linked to my actions.

The other big thing was that before the counselling I couldn't shake the sadness. If there was sadness in the world, other people's sadness, I couldn't shake it off. It was like a shroud over me. Whereas now I can look at it and be moved certainly – I'd like to think I haven't become cold or detached – but I've had to detach myself more than I used to. I had to realise that me being miserable was not going to help the Rwandans and it certainly wasn't going to help my family. Whilst I still empathise with others' pain now I can move on from it.

The abuse took my childhood from me, that innocence. That feeling that the world is a good place and a family is a safe place to be. Because your childhood is your foundation for life if there are one or two bits that are a bit wonky, then things that you build on it are askew. I feel that you have to be ever vigilant. I'm not hyper about the boys any more, but I would be very keen on giving them skills to deal with situations.

The abuse also took from me for awhile, and can still do, the most intimate and precious moments for Anthony and myself. I find that very hard. How dare he! After twenty years he can still be there. But if it happens now Anthony knows the signs. He'd say "you're thinking of it now, aren't you?" and he'd say, "fine, forget about it , we can come back to it another time." I don't feel if it happens that it's my fault.

I didn't tackle my abuser when I met him when I was twenty-five, I was just too stunned. I look on that time now as maybe opening the can of worms a little bit and shutting it again. About a month into the counselling, my counsellor asked me if I would like to do anything about it. One of the reasons that I wanted to tackle him was because I felt a duty to other children that he might be in contact with now. If I maintained a vow of silence I would be in part guilty for any ongoing abuse they might be suffering.

I read that Bishop Forristal, in Kilkenny, was in charge of a committee for dealing with allegations of clerical abuse. So I wrote him a letter. He replied and then phoned me. He couldn't have been nicer and he set the ball in motion. He asked me if I wanted to track the priest down. I knew he was in Australia now. They tracked him down and then the Bishop wrote again and told me where he was and asked did I want to take it further. He kept in touch with me all the way. The sense of power I had was incredible.

She has brought these letters with her and we stop to look at them. She also shows me an old family photograph taken during one of the summers of her childhood. In the picture is her abuser.

When I think of the abuser I still feel absolute revulsion. I don't hate him because it would take too much energy. I feel he has taken up so much of my energy and my precious first years with Joe especially. I wouldn't waste hate.

Writing was a great help to me in the healing process and I wrote a letter to him

Her voice trembles as she reads and she is never far from tears. She breaks down several times.

"I don't want to waste any more of my energy on you. You don't deserve any consideration. On the other hand if I felt I was protecting other children then I would do something. In the meantime I'm trying to know that none of your carry-on was my fault and I'm doing my level best to know that I am good and worthwhile.

"You are pathetic. I wish you many hours of torment, but I don't want to waste any energy feeling anything towards you. I don't know what I would do if I ever met you again. Spitting at you comes to mind and that is like something a child would do. And as I said before I don't think you ever thought I would grow up. For a long time I blocked out everything that you did to me.

"When you visited us that time after Daddy died I honestly think that you had conveniently forgotten lots of things as well. Mainly I think that you believed that I would never grow up to be an adult. Well I did, and despite your *actions I'm a fairly sound one. I hate to give you the satisfaction of saying this to you because you don't deserve to have this power over me, but you've also made some of the most precious parts of my life very tarnished. You're a sleaze, a creep and lower than life itself. For a long time I blamed Mammy and Daddy for not minding me enough but as I have begun to think of those times more I now realise where they were.*

"How dare you take away the trust of so many people. I would love to see you put away where you would never see the real world again especially any one with children in it."

That sums it up. I actually sent that letter and that felt good.

The tribunal of the Catholic Church in Australia wrote back to me. Bishop Forristal would get the letters first and then he would write or phone me. I thought it was so thoughtful. He would prepare me by letting me know that there was going to be a letter in the post. It was such a small thing but it mattered so much.

Then he phoned me to say there was a letter on its way with a letter from the abuser. When I got the envelope the outside letter was from Bishop Forristal, then there was an inside letter from the Australian Bishop and then inside that again was the letter from the abuser. They handled it so sensitively. So I actually got a letter from him.

He wrote . . .

"Dear Molly,

I write to express my deep regret at the way I treated you when I worked for your family. I abused your person. In doing that I also abused a sacred trust of you as a young child in a relationship with an adult. For these wrongs and all the pain and harm I have caused in your life I am deeply sorry and now want to offer you a sincere apology. I only hope that perhaps in some little way this letter might lessen that pain and make your future years more peaceful. My bishop has suspended me from all priestly duties indefinitely and advised me to go and get some professional help. I have accepted his advice. Finally Molly, I wish that your future years and those of your family be filled with God's peace and love and that His undoubted love for you may help to heal the wounds I caused you. In sorrow and with deep regret,

Yours sincerely . . . "

I felt a bit of relief. He's in therapy now somewhere. I had to send them legal documents with formal allegations.

I also got a letter from the Bishop in Australia . . .

"Dear Mrs – ,

Thank you for having the courage to come forward and inform us of your abuse by Father X. As Bishop Forristal has informed you Father X has admitted his offence and has been removed from active ministry. He left the diocese last week for therapy and his future ministry will depend on the results of the therapy and whether a place can be found which will minimise his contact with children.

"Father X has indicated that he is going to send you an apology via Bishop Forristal. He has been warned not to approach you directly by mail or in person. If he should do this please inform us immediately."

Those few words about keeping him away from

children meant as much to me as any of the rest. That was what I wanted. Not to have him locked up in servitude but just kept away from children. He had actually been a parish priest out in the bush. The only priest for thousands of miles, so you can imagine the pool of resources he would have had if he was still engaged in abuse.

I'm glad that my past hurts weren't added to by me being mishandled. It would have been terrible if he had denied it. It was just a sense of relief. The feeling of power was great – by writing a letter I can make a difference. I thought "God yes, I wrote and I got him suspended and everything." It's actually a very insignificant part of my healing and it wasn't a kind of vendetta. I didn't want him to have that power over me and it worked.

I've had to learn to trust my instincts again, to be in tune with them again. I blocked them out for so long. I'm regaining confidence in trusting my gut.

I also realise that the use of words can make a difference to how you feel. Saying "I'm a victim of abuse", means for me that I'm still in his power, but I'm a *survivor* of abuse. All the tactics I learned to help me block out things I actually needed those so that I could survive my adolescence.

I've also learned that you need to have the confidence to know where to go for help and not be afraid to look for it. People are there for you. Some books are also great. I found Louise Haye's book *The Power is Within You* a great help. It's also important to keep looking until you get the right help. I can always go back to the Rape Crisis Centre if I want. I feel very lucky that I read that newspaper article and then that I had the courage to take it a step further and Anthony was there to help me to take that step. Anthony and I have come through it and the tapestry of our life is so much richer, not because of it but for what we've learned from it.

DEREK

DEREK

***"From the outside it might have looked like
a breakdown but for me in a sense it
was a breakthrough."***

He is now fifty and married with three grown children. Of medium height, he is powerfully built with long greying hair in a pony-tail. He wears a dark green sweater and carries a leather shoulder bag. Now a successful artist his voice still retains the accent of several years of public schooling in England.

I meet him off the train and we travel to my house where we settle ourselves on the couch with cups of tea. He is tense but visibly relaxes after some time.

(Some of the names and locations in this story have been changed to protect people's identity.)

Growing up in the forties and the fifties children were abused almost as a matter of course – physically and emotionally. I think people seem to have forgotten this. I grew up in ostensibly a very privileged background. My father was a senior physician in a big hospital and we lived in a big house in the middle of the city. He was never a very rich doctor but there were a lot of the trappings of wealth. I was brought up by a nanny and we had a cook and two maids as well. That wasn't unusual in a professional house in the forties.

I grew up in an ambience where children were to be seen and not heard, and if they were heard they were hit. I didn't see my parents at all when I was a small child. I was in the nursery and there was a nanny. I suppose I was looked at occasionally, or produced on some suitable social occasion. I don't have any memories of my parents, except on holiday, until I started going to primary school and then my father would drive me to school on his way to the hospital.

I had one brother who was six years older than me and he was already at boarding school by the time I was aware of him. He was sent to boarding school at the age of eight. That was routine at the time. There were kids in my first boarding school who were seven. They'd be sent up from the country, or their parents were in the forces or out in the colonies. It was absolutely routine in the colonies for children to be sent back to the British Isles to go to prep school from the age of six or seven. All of this was totally taken for granted.

I don't remember much before four or five. As was usual for that class at the time I spent most of the time in the nursery with my nanny. My mother didn't breast feed me. Although she was a well-built woman she used to say she hadn't enough milk for a sparrow. I think she was probably discouraged anyway because it wasn't fashionable. I know from my family that I was in a cot from the word go, bottle-fed at absolutely regulation intervals, never before or after the allotted time, and that was the way of it.

My first nanny was sacked when I was nearly two because they discovered that she was beating me whenever I cried. Ironically it was my brother who actually said "oh, nanny is beating the baby." Apparently whenever I bawled as a child she used to give me a good thump and put me back in the cot. I remember there was a net over the top of the cot to keep me in. I remember holding the bars and always trying to climb out.

My second nanny came along when I was about two and I suppose her presence was the dominant one in my early childhood. I loved her and feared her, all mixed up together. She was seventeen when she came to us. She'd been to some sort of training college for nannies. She was a big strapping country girl and her solution to any problem was a good wallop. This was the way children were brought up at that time. The philosophy was "spare the rod and spoil the child." If the child was bold, which was basically doing anything that drew attention to itself, give it a good wallop. She used to say things like "I'll tan the hide off you", "I'll knock you into the middle of next week."

I suppose my first memories of my parents were when I was about three or four and we were on holiday down in the West of Ireland. We usually went for the month of August. My father would go fishing and my mother was an artist so she would be off painting. So my brother, his friend, my nanny and me were left together.

The holidays were a mixture of fear and fun because my brother bullied me. He was six years older than me, which is a lot at that stage. He was so much stronger and so much larger than me.

I don't remember talking to my parents much. The only memory of real communication was with my father when he started driving me to school in the mornings when I was about five. I only really started to know him then. I'd be questioning him the whole time about things. I liked that but I was terrified of him as well.

You've got to throw your mind back fifty years, I grew up in an incredibly formal household. Since Princess Diana's death people have been talking about the appalling emotional coldness of the Windsors. That's the way I was brought up. I grew up under a regime where emotions and feelings were never discussed or displayed, voices were never raised. There were no arguments. There were no fights. Good manners, politeness, no matter what.

At the same time my father was a very deeply compassionate man with regard to his patients. He treated hundreds of people for free because they couldn't afford to pay. There was a constant stream of people to the front door of the house in the afternoon. That was where he had his consultations when he wasn't in the hospital. Everybody had to be quiet. Not a squeak during the afternoons.

Even though he was a caring and compassionate man he did not spend much time with us children. It just wasn't the way children were brought up.

My mother and father were passionately in love with each other. After they died I was going through a lot of papers and there was a whole stash of letters to each other when they were first married. I started reading some of them and then I just stopped because they were getting far too personal and far too intimate. I just felt that I was completely intruding on them, on something incredibly private and precious. The only thing that I did sort of follow through with some interest were letters from my mother to my father begging that they shouldn't have children. She didn't want any because she felt it would spoil their relationship.

I don't ever remember them being demonstrative with one another. I don't ever remember them holding hands. I mean, a kiss on the cheek and that was it. I don't ever remember them hugging anybody. I certainly was never hugged. I remember as a child when we were out in the country on long walks sometimes my father would pick me up and carry me if I got tired. It was great.

Dad was the ultimate authority figure so there was an awful lot of fear mixed up with all this. The worst threat was "I'll tell your father." I got slapped by my nanny every day of the week but that didn't frighten nearly as much as "I'll tell your father." He was a very big man and very gruff in his manner. He himself found it extremely difficult to express his emotions.

I didn't really know my older brother. I only knew him in the holidays. I was afraid of him but he was also a hero. He was very gifted with his hands and could make balsa wood aeroplanes that flew and model boats that sailed. Unfortunately for him, he wasn't terribly bright intellectually. I think my father had great expectations of his older son and was a bit taken aback when he turned out to be a bit slow.

I think my brother, God bless him, had a hard time living up to our father's expectations. I remember on one occasion he said "well you know every single thing that I did no matter what it was, Dad always suggested an improvement." That was typical of my dad. I was very fortunate, I was the bright one and I had no difficulties with school at all. I did well with very little effort. But I never ever, ever remember my father saying "well done" – not once.

When I was in boarding school in England I did extremely well in my A Levels and got an A 1 in one subject, which was reckoned to be virtually impossible. When I came back joyously and told my father he just sort of went "hmm, why didn't you get an A 1 in the other subject?"

It wasn't until I was an adult that I ever got unconditional approval from him. It was my first major bronze sculpture and he was completely stunned. I was thirty-six and I remember thinking at the time "phew, finally I got there. Finally he approves of me."

From my earliest childhood there was always plenty of paint and paper around and I was always painting. It was totally encouraged. We did some painting in the primary school I was at. It was fairly go-ahead from that point of view and my mother actually came there and taught painting for a bit. There was always plasticine and modelling clay and that kind of stuff. So for me happiness came out of the end of a brush. From earliest childhood that was my main source of happiness.

When we went to the West of Ireland on holidays we took two cars. My brother and my nanny invariably went in my father's car and I went in my mother's little car. We took the two cars because my father used to go fishing while my mother went off painting.

Those trips down in the car were the closest I ever got to my mother. We used to chat and I enjoyed the trip but my mother was a depressive and a very complex person. I remember growing up with her always saying "why can't you be normal, why can't you be like everybody else, why must you be different? Why can't you be like your brother?"

I think she wanted me to be a good, quiet little well-behaved boy who stayed in his place and didn't make too much noise. It took me a long time to realise that I was brought up in a complete double-bind. My mother saying "you must be good, you must behave, you must be normal" and then my father insisting that I should be exceptional "you must be the best, you must come first, you must get a first." So there were a lot of confusing messages.

Through all of this I wasn't a miserable child. According to one woman who was like a second mother to me, I was "imaginatively wicked". She used to tell me that if there was some devilment to be got up to, I'd be up to it. This woman was the mother of my two closest childhood friends, with whom I spent a lot of time. She was like a substitute mother. She was warm and she talked to us and made real contact. We were very rambunctious kids. Don't get the impression that I was a sort of sad little waif or something, absolutely not.

Then, when I was just nine I went to boarding school and that was a nightmare, mainly because of the headmaster. It was awful. When I complained to my mother about the headmaster and the fact that I was being beaten so often she just said "oh don't be silly. His bark is worse than his bite." My father thought that beating was a good thing as he had spent some time in the colonies where flogging was a routine punishment.

The thing was that at my prep school I was a misfit.

A lot of the kids had English parents who were in the forces or in the colonies. It was a dumping ground for the children of privileged parents. I'm sure that I was one of the most Irish and I had a different accent to the other kids. Also I was a city dweller, whereas a lot of them came from large country houses and they were into horses and all of that kind of stuff. None of which meant anything to me.

The headmaster was a total, raving psychotic. He should never have been let near children. He had complete favourites and complete pariahs. He was a man of appallingly brutal temper, absolutely terrifying. Anything would trigger him into a rage and he would literally go black in the face, froth at the mouth and his cheeks would puff in and out. He would hit, kick or beat whatever was in range. There were about half a dozen of us who were his complete *béte noir* because we drew attention to ourselves.

For instance, one unfortunate boy committed the cardinal sin of having biscuits in his locker along with his books. The headmaster did one of his periodic locker searches to see that nobody was keeping anything they shouldn't have in their lockers. He found that this lad had a packet of biscuits and he dragged him out of bed in the middle of the night. He hauled the poor guy, more or less literally by the hair, across the yard and then beat him until he got tired from beating him. The kid was about ten or eleven.

I'm not joking, I remember it vividly, that kid had bruises from his knees to his shoulder blades which stayed there for three or four months. That's how savage the beating was. He beat him with a big rubber gym shoe. The kid was left in a dreadful state. He didn't get any medical help. He was barely able to move for days. No complaint was ever made to the parents.

I was utterly miserable in my prep school. Anybody who was outside a certain norm of behaviour was an oddity. If you were musical or artistic you were definitely considered strange. I was brought up with music and art as the two things that were the main sources of pleasure in my life so I was definitely considered to be an oddity.

I was one of the half dozen or so pariahs in the school who were ostracised by most of the kids. The headmaster was so terrifying that nobody would want to associate with anybody who was regularly a target of his wrath. In fact there were a couple of us who were constant targets of bullying for other boys just because they knew they could get away with it.

We had some very peculiar people as masters. I don't know where they managed to dredge them up. There was one master who decided he was going to beat me. Before he did so he made me go and change into my sports gear, shorts and a singlet. Then when I appeared before him he made me remove my gear and started to sort of feel me up and fondle me. I remember that didn't particularly shock me, but what did was the fact that he was planning to beat me on my bare backside. I remember whipping my shorts back on again and saying "oh you're not allowed beat me on my bare backside, only the headmaster is allowed do that." I don't know where I got that idea from but it worked.

The headmaster himself was a very strange man and his wife, I later heard, was an alcoholic. On occasion the headmaster would say to whoever the duty master was

"I'll put the boys to bed tonight." Then he might say "right, I'll give the boys a shower." Then we'd all go and have a shower. We'd be in the games changing rooms while the headmaster looked after us and patted bottoms here and there and that sort of thing. If you were one of the lucky ones he patted your bottom, that was infinitely to be preferred to the kind of pounding that some of us got most of the time.

I got thrashed by him with monotonous regularity. It was taken for granted. I had no cuts because the gym shoe doesn't break the skin. A cane might, but the gym shoe was extremely painful and it didn't actually cut the skin because it was wide and flat.

In the summer, if we got sunburn, the headmaster would come around. Not the matron or the assistant matron but the headmaster would come around and rub Calamine lotion on our backs. It was very much a privilege to be one of the ones who had Calamine lotion rubbed on them, because it meant that day that he probably approved of you. In winter it was Vick into one's chest. So it was a bit kinky but I don't suppose it was too bad.

The thing with him was that you never knew from one minute to the next just what was going to happen. I remember on one occasion I was called to his study and he gave me this long lecture praising me for all sorts of wonderful things that I had done and he then he said "but you are a bloody little arse, McCarthy, I'm going to have to knock some sense into you" and thereupon he beat the shite out of me. Then on another occasion I was summoned to his study. He was standing there with a football corner flag-pole in his hand. It looked like it was going to be the beating of all time. Then he put it down, told me my grandmother had just died, and hugged me.

That was a surprise.

My experience of school being brutally violent was absolutely the experience of so many children growing up in Ireland in the forties and fifties.

Even when I was sent for piano lessons at the age of four my teacher's technique was quite simple – if you made a mistake you got a wallop across the back of the hands with the edge of the ruler. To this day I can't play the piano.

By the time I was in prep school the sexual abuse from my brother had already started. It had started when I was about nine. I always remembered it, I never forgot it. It has struck me that my situation in the general context of what happens in sexual abuse cases is probably unusual because there was no violence associated with it.

There had been a lot of physical violence as well as emotional coldness in the background of my life, but that was just taken for granted when I was a child. I suppose looking back now I would have been classified as a battered baby, being thumped as an infant, for God's sake. Then there were the regular beatings both from my nanny and when I was in prep school. That was completely the norm as far as I understood it.

But the actual sexual abuse when it came on was not surrounded by violence at all. But premature sexualisation, no matter what form it comes in, is damaging. The first sort of disquiet I remember feeling around my brother was when we were on summer holidays down in the West of Ireland, I would have only been about eight. I suppose he was already a teenager of about fourteen. He was already sexually mature at that age.

For whatever reason he got in the bath with me. I just remember I'd never been aware of him sexually before, but all of a sudden there was my brother sitting in the bath playing with himself. He had what looked to me like this absolutely enormous erection and this great mass of black pubic hair which for some reason terrified me. I didn't say anything. He didn't do anything to me at that stage but that is the first image that I have of something that was sexually traumatic. Even talking about it now at this late stage it still disturbs me.

We stop. He is sighing deeply, clearly upset. There is a long pause. He gathers himself and continues.

I suppose the abuse really got going when I was about nine, during the summer holidays. We were staying in a small family hotel and he and I shared a room. There was no violence. He cajoled me and said effectively "this is something that's fun that you can do. Come and do it to me." Again I can see the image very clearly of him sitting there and this colossal erection and all this very threatening black pubic hair curled around his genitals. He insisted that I masturbate him and then he ejaculated and that was absolutely terrifying. I had no idea what was happening. I just remember the awful feeling of this stuff all over my hands. It was sticky and smelly. That was fairly traumatic.

At the same time there was the feeling that this was something very adult, secret and serious and totally taboo. It was like I was part of some very kind of special secret life that he had. At the same time I felt in myself that I was doing something very wicked. Whatever this was I must never ever, ever talk about it. He said "don't tell anybody or I'll kill you." Those were the words he used. Obviously he didn't mean them but he was very much bigger than me and very powerfully built. He was a runner and a climber and so was very, very strong. He was a bit of a bully.

My parents never knew what was going on. They were off doing their own thing and my brother and I were left to our own devices.

I felt very, very confused about this sexual activity. On the one hand there was the illicit thrill of it because it was something very obviously adult, but at the same time I found it terrifying and physically revolting. He also started masturbating me. Being only nine or ten I was prematurely sexualised.

For the next few years my brother would regularly use me as a sexual partner one way or another during the holidays. He would get me to masturbate him. Once he got me to sodomise him. I mean he got *me* to sodomise *him*, which was quite odd. God knows why I did it because it was terrifying and just awful. He never actually sodomised me but once he made me suck him . . .

Again we must stop. Derek takes many deep breaths. The memories seem to be almost suffocating him. He cannot speak for some minutes and then continues with difficulty.

I'll tell you one of the things that terrified me, and this is a very particular and horrible detail, the taste of his sperm in my mouth. Repulsive. The size of his penis in my hand was totally terrifying, it was just so big, so huge. I mean I was only nine and had not matured physically. Things like that were absolutely awful and in fact they are some of the hardest memories. I was so confused and frightened and in many ways repulsed, physically repulsed by the whole business of sex with another male.

Yet, the fact that somebody wanted me, the fact that I was needed by someone for whatever reason was a powerful incentive to do whatever he wanted me to do. When you've been brought up with nannies and packed off to boarding school at the first possible opportunity, you get quite a strong message that basically you are not wanted. You're a nuisance. So this was what you deserved and the fact that somebody wanted you was very powerful, very seductive.

It's a very distressing memory still. The funny thing is I've been around this experience and worked through it consciously for six years and it's still very upsetting. The only way that I can rationalise my involvement in it is because for the first time in my life I felt somebody needed and wanted me. That was the sad thing. That was really painful.

I felt the abuse was my fault for doing it. It was something bad. I was doing something bad. Anything to do with sex or anything like that was absolutely taboo.

At my prep school, although it wasn't a Catholic school, there was still loads of religion. Unlike Catholic schools we had to learn vast chunks of the Bible off by heart, a verse a day. There were prayers morning and evening and church on Sunday and all that sort of stuff. Also having had a Catholic nanny I had a very, very deep sense of sin. I had been told since earliest memory that all Protestants go to hell anyway because they're heretics.

My nanny was not so blatant as to say this to me but she had brothers and sisters who did. I used to go and spend some of the summer holidays with my nanny down on her family farm. Her brothers and sisters and other Catholic children that I met would all say the same thing "oh, well of course you're a Protestant, you're going to hell anyway."

I had a very strong sense of sin and what I was doing was wrong, even though it was my brother who was doing it. I felt desperately guilty. Shamed. Disgusted. Unclean.

Then when I was thirteen I was sent away to boarding school in England. I remember clearly the first two questions I asked when I got there. The first was "how often do you get beaten?" They looked at me with shock and they said "oh you don't get beaten unless you've done something really bad." I said "oh, well how often would that be? Would you get beaten once or twice a week or what?". "Oh, no, no, no. Heavens, no. You might get beaten once a year."

He claps his hand together with delight . . .

Brilliant!

My second question was "do you have to eat the food?" The food in my prep school had been so repulsive that I regularly got beaten for not eating it. I just couldn't swallow it. I got beaten once for vomiting at the table and another time I got beaten for vomiting during prayers in the evening. Apparently I should have known that I was going to vomit and I should have left the room. I actually vomited all over my Bible, which was unforgivable.

So, when I asked about eating the food they said "you don't have to eat anything if you don't want to." Wonderful! Those were my two first questions.

I hadn't been in the school for more than a week when I was visited in bed by a senior boy. He wanted me to masturbate him, which I did, and he masturbated me. This was a familiar scenario.

When I was about fourteen, I was becoming a very devout and guilt-ridden Christian. I remember I swore to God that I would never ever masturbate again, and if I ever did, may God strike me dead. My vow lasted for at least two weeks . . . God didn't seem to mind too much. So there I was an adolescent like any other amongst a whole crowd of adolescent boys, still riddled with guilt and sin. But I hadn't been struck dead.

Masturbation amongst the boys in the school was absolutely rife. The building used to shake at night.

He laughs.

I mean there were fifty boys in a dormitory. A big long room like a stable with horse boxes along the side of it, waist high cubicles. Boys didn't seem to mind too much if other boys saw them. It was not uncommon for older boys to come to the beds of younger boys. It didn't happen much to me. We were all adolescent boys with no physical outlets except sport, cold baths and masturbation.

By the time he'd left boarding school my brother had stopped abusing me. I think he'd discovered the delights of girlfriends and he didn't need me any more. He was pretty much out of my life by then, being much older.

I remember my big ambition was to grow taller than

him, which I did. Because then I'd be stronger than him and he'd never be able to beat me up again.

Whilst he was abusing me I suppose my main feelings towards him were fear. But I'm not sure what I felt about anything at that time. I don't remember having any feelings at all except maybe ones of fear or excitement. Feelings weren't felt. Emotions were never expressed. Feelings were something that well-behaved people didn't have.

The boarding school in England was a complete change from my prep school. Everything that had got me into trouble at the prep school, got me acclaim at public school. Being an extrovert, a musician, an artist, all of that was approved of and put me amongst the elite. I just lived for acting, music and art. I was also fortunate that school work came very easily to me so I was in the A stream all the way through.

Also as I grew I became fairly strong. I was on my house rugger team. Although I didn't care for games very much, I wasn't bad at them. I wasn't really very good but I was acceptable.

As I said when I was fourteen or fifteen I was a very fervent, anxious and guilt-ridden Christian. I used to go to Communion every morning at seven o'clock. I was in the choir so I spent a lot of time in the chapel. I suppose I was looking desperately for some kind of security.

We used to always have a visiting preacher during Lent, this was Church of England, of course. One Lent we had this very charismatic Protestant monk who talked to us every morning in chapel. At the end of it he said that he would hold confession. Jaws dropped and eyes opened. He said "don't think confession is only something for Catholics, Protestants can confess as well.

I will be holding confession and anybody who wants to come and see me can do so."

I went to see him and I confessed everything that I could think of that I'd ever done or that had caused me any hint or twinge of guilt. So I was with him a long time. I told him all the stuff about sex with my brother – on which he did not comment. He didn't comment on anything he just listened to it all, gave me absolution and then he told me to go away and not to worry. I walked out of there just feeling all of a sudden unburdened. I remember feeling that I was literally floating on air. It was an extraordinary feeling.

The next year we had an even more amazing man. He was an English vicar from a very troubled area in London. He came and talked about his own history which was a history of alcoholism and fairly depraved sex and all that sort of thing – until he had his vocation. He was telling our whole school of six hundred randy teenagers about his own problems with masturbation. I thought "oh my God, a priest talking about it. He said that terrible word." So gradually the incredible black layers of misery and guilt that I was carrying around began to loosen up a bit and it began to seem to me that perhaps sex was a natural thing.

Just before I had gone off to public school in England my father had taken me into his study one day and said "now, Derek I've got to tell you about the facts of life." At this stage I thought I knew most of the facts of life through my brother. He started saying things like "oh well you know at your age you'll find that your penis gives you a certain amount of pleasure." He went on to explain to me about masturbation. I remember sitting there looking at the ceiling and thinking "oh my God, he's not going to tell me about this. This is so embarrassing. I can't tell him I know and I can't tell him how I know." He said "don't believe all the nonsense that people say. It's a perfectly natural thing it won't do you any harm". I remember thinking "what! It's perfectly natural! How can he say that?" Because it seemed to me a terribly wicked thing to be doing – masturbation. And sex with my brother was twice as bad.

One of the things that happened in public school was that the choir went on a school tour to France and stayed in private houses. I was madly smitten with the daughter of one family. I was there for three or four days and we ended up sleeping together. We were about sixteen. We slept together, we were in bed together but we did not have sexual intercourse. It was incredibly innocent when I look back on it. I had no sisters and like many a public school boy of my generation I had the most incredibly romantic notions about women. They were completely alien creatures. They inhabited a different world altogether.

Where girls were concerned my mind was completely split. When I started kissing girls and all that kind of stuff, by some miracle it came with no guilt attached. I don't know why but it just seemed to be acceptable. Whereas the involvement with my brother was absolutely a taboo thing.

So this French girl and I spent the night together and it was incredible. It was unbelievably blissful. I don't think we slept a wink. But I thought I was completely, totally, madly and hopelessly in love with her. I wrote to her for about two years afterwards but I didn't see her again for about six years by which time we had moved totally into different realms. That was the first time I ever slept with a girl and it was like a revelation. It was totally trauma-free and beautiful. An amazing, lovely, blissful, happy experience.

When I went to college I suppose I was quite fortunate in that my relationships with girls were actually fairly easy, certainly at the early stages. But once I began on any regular basis to have sex, this was the late sixties, there would be demons in the background. The whole business of the abuse with my brother never actually surfaced in a traumatic way but I never forgot it. It was sort of shut away in a totally separate compartment. It was completely sealed. It was somewhere else.

When I say there were demons in the background what I mean is sex became compulsive. Looking back now I can see that this was a frantic need for approval. A frantic need for love in any shape or form or from any source. I was desperately looking for affection particularly because, as I've said, I grew up in an ambience where affection was simply absent and love was never demonstrated.

So sex for me, more than anything else, was a way of gaining affection. When I say it was fairly compulsive I felt driven to be some kind of a super stud. Anything, anything to be loved.

I was compulsive in all sorts of different behaviours. I was still in college and very much involved in acting, music and art, but particularly with acting. People who reckon they're going to be actors (which is what I reckoned I was going to be) are often people with deep emotional needs. I was always acting. Even off-stage I was acting all the time.

When I say I was acting all the time I mean it quite literally. There was never a moment when I wasn't in some sense putting on an act. I was a compulsive actor. I was compulsively trying to be funny, trying to amuse people. It must have been hell to be around me.

Then, the first time that I did seriously fall in love with a girl in college I stopped acting. That was to me very significant. All of a sudden I didn't need to act anymore and I gave up – stopped. I think she saw clean through the act.

This was in the late sixties and she had been through the whole dope and acid scene. I hadn't. The extraordinary thing was that for the first month or two when she and I made love I had what would be called a "near death" experience many times. I would have a more or less "out of body" experience. I found myself whizzing down a kind of a tunnel, a big revolving tunnel, into light – into a pool of unbounded light and a feeling of complete and utter bliss. A feeling of not actually being in the presence of a Being but *being*. This happened several times after orgasm.

I think what was happening was a kind of spontaneous transcendence. My whole system was just really settling down into an inner quietness or something like that. I had become interested in yoga and more or less any sort of a spiritual path that did not seem to be encumbered with huge amounts of pain, suffering and guilt. By that stage I knew that what I was looking for in life was the one thing that had been significantly absent up to now – serenity. That was the word used at the time. There were some people who seemed to have a quality of serenity about them.

I also realised that the kind of incredibly compulsive extrovert, acting, manic behaviour that I had been living with from about the age of four up until the time of this relationship was neurotic. I just knew that I had been very, very unhappy, and now all of a sudden here I was and there was happiness. Happiness and spirituality and serenity all seemed to belong together.

My girlfriend decided to go to the US and I went over to join her for a while but things were different and after a while I realised that the relationship was over. Whilst I was in the States I got into drugs in a fairly big way and when I came back to Ireland I continued to use them. I was smoking dope all the time interspersed with acid, speed and all the hallucinogenic and soft drugs. I actually drank very little alcohol, I couldn't handle it. It just upset my digestion too much.

I went into a very depressed state and was in psychiatric care. In spite of all of that, the recognition of the abusive sexual relationship with my brother, didn't actually dawn on me until much, much later. It was just so completely sealed off. It was like this black area in the middle of my psyche that I just couldn't deal with. I couldn't express it and couldn't talk about it. I never forgot it but it was always in its own compartment.

The funny thing was although the relationship with my girlfriend had been extraordinarily intense, physically she was as screwed up as I was. She hadn't recognised it at that stage but she had been sexually abused by her father. She only rediscovered this years later, but at that time she had all sorts of hang-ups around sex. Our physical relationship was the most problematic area for her.

I continued being heavily into drugs for three years after our break-up. This was the high hippie era and at the time it didn't seem particularly unusual. During those three years I had about fifty sexual partners. The philosophy of the time was basically "if you can't be with the one you love, love the one you're with." If that sounds like a lot of sex it wasn't by the standards of the time. To me sex was a way of being loved. Being super stud was another act, it was another performance really.

What got me off drugs was Transcendental Meditation. I was working in the theatre after leaving college. One of my colleagues, a musician, was noticeably serene, calm, quiet and efficient. All the things I wasn't. It turned out he was a TM teacher. I was very cynical about it, but eventually I decided to learn. It was the turning point in my life.

My anxiety eased, my health improved, and I no longer felt the need for drugs. For the first time ever I felt "at home" in myself. The need to be putting on an act faded away. The meditation gave me back a sense of direction, so my life started to get back on track. I left the theatre and trained as a sculptor.

During the course of my involvement with meditation I met my wife. She was meditating as well. When I saw her it was love at first sight. Absolutely, totally. I was knocked out. The nice thing was that she and I had a very, very easy physical relationship, probably for the first time ever. All those compulsive needs to be some kind of a super stud just weren't relevant any more.

I think my anxieties around sex had been coupled with a very poor self-image. The anxiety was "would I be a good enough lover? Would I be adequate? Would the girl have sufficiently numerous and devastating orgasms in order to want me?" Sex was a means for me to get love.

But from the first the physical relationship between myself and my wife was absolutely trouble free. I was twenty-six when I got married and we have three children. We're still married and it is twenty-three years later. Obviously like many relationships we have had our ups and downs and there have been a couple of moments when I've strayed from the straight and narrow. There were three occasions when I made love with other women. Maybe it had something to do with me turning forty and all that kind of stuff, perhaps feeling insecure. Whatever the reason. I regret it.

I think at times when the marriage was going through difficulties, my self-esteem was low and I would probably blame myself for the problems. We were also both very intensely involved with the raising of our children. There was one thing for sure, my children were not going to be sent to boarding school. Neither were they going to have absentee parents.

About six years ago my old girlfriend came back from the US to visit us. By this time she was in her mid-forties and she was in therapy. It was only then that I learned that she had been abused. It had taken until then for her memories to surface. She had been abused by her father when she was a child.

It was only when she started describing all the various symptoms in her psychological make-up that were attributed to the abuse that something suddenly snapped in me and I recognised all those symptoms in myself. Then the whole thing reconnected. All of a sudden all of the feelings that had been shut off, bottled up, packed away came pouring out – the sexual abuse from my brother, the violence of my childhood and also the violence and abuse at prep school. It was like all those emotions were suddenly reconnected – all the fear and guilt, all the anxiety, all the misery. Something just snapped. It was like a trickle of sand which becomes an avalanche. It wasn't as though I had ever forgotten it but at the same time it had been in the deep freeze. Now all of a sudden it was back and it produced a sort of psychic collapse.

My entire life, looking back over it, seemed to be nothing more than an attempt to cope and to cover over that trauma. Everything that I had done, from very early childhood on, seemed to me in retrospect to be a construct to hide the blackness at the core of my being. This was the guilt and shame and the sense of awful sin with regard to the whole sexual thing. I now think that the abusive relationship with my brother was only a symptom of a deeper emptiness which was the absence of love and affection as a very small child. The fact that I was even involved in abuse with my brother was a symptom of an earlier problem.

So when this happened about six years ago it seemed as though suddenly there was nothing there any more. It was as though all the music, all the acting, all the art, everything – was purely an attempt to cover over what John Bradshaw calls "the hole in the soul" – down which hole everything had disappeared. I looked back and saw everything I had done in my life as being an attempt to fill in a lack at the core of my being. It was all a distress call saying "please love me", "please show me some affection", "please give me some attention." Pathetic, isn't it?

The lack I suppose was just the lack of love in early infancy. Or maybe it was to do with the battering I received as an infant. This was amplified all the way up by the brutality. There was a stage after the breakdown when if somebody had called my name, I would not have known who they were talking to. The physical entity was still there but everything I identified with as being me suddenly seemed pointless and worthless. I had always identified not with who I was but with what I did.

From the outside it might have looked like a breakdown but for me in a sense it was a breakthrough. It was a fairly appalling realisation to feel that everything that I had done, everything, had been an attempt to fill in the "hole in my soul". I saw everything I had done as worthless. My entire life just dissolved and me with it. My relationship with my wife and children seemed to be a sham. My identity, my personality, everything just went. There was nothing left. There was just the continuation of the physical body. Fortunately there was also a continuum of inner silence to which the years of meditation had given me access.

I feel strongly if it had not been for my children and the fact that I was meditating I might have committed suicide then. The meditation was a resource which somehow seemed to go deeper than the level of the emotional trauma. There was a part of me that said "hey, come on you can survive this. This is not the end." There was a very suicidal element in that collapse of the psyche. All meaning was gone. I just wanted to disappear and sleep forever.

I rang up the Rape Crisis Centre and said "look, I think I need help. What do you suggest?" They recommended a couple of people but it turned out that they had waiting lists of at least a year. There seemed to be so few people dealing with the problem of abuse, particularly for male victims. I rang the Rape Crisis Centre again several times and they were wonderfully supportive and extremely helpful. They told me there was a book I might like to read called *The Courage to Heal*. They said it was mainly aimed at women but it would probably help.

The book is a therapeutic manual. You work your way slowly through it and the authors recommend keeping a journal. So I started writing a journal which is something that I'd never ever been able to do before. Suddenly I found that this journal became my main occupation and I was writing probably a couple of thousand words a day. Gradually I was working through the book and writing the journal. It brought a lot of stuff to the surface.

I read it to my wife in the evenings and we were going through a wonderful re-enlivening of our relationship. All of a sudden light was let into an area that had been dark for most of my life and there was a wonderful six months of revitalisation between the two of us. Now all sorts of areas in my psyche were clear and open that had never been visible before because they were under lock and key.

In the course of working through all this it transpired that my wife had also been sexually abused as a child and I think what had happened to her was much more traumatic than what happened to me. She then had a very severe breakdown after I had mine, and she is still in the process of dealing with it.

I worked with the book for a couple of years and then had one session with an analyst which was utterly hopeless. Then I found an excellent therapist and I went to him for some months. That worked very well. We covered a lot of ground and a lot of stuff came back to the surface going right back to my earliest infancy.

Nowadays I would say that the demons are pretty much exorcised. Sexually troubling images still come to mind, which I think are associated with the abuse. I don't know if one is ever really clear of it. The wounds heal but the scars remain.

I've been asked "aren't you extremely angry with your brother?" Strangely, I found that I could only really connect to anger if I thought of what he did with me being done to any of my children. Then I suddenly find a huge anger. But with regard to myself I find it quite hard to feel angry. Six years ago when I was first going through it, quite a lot of anger came up. But my background and upbringing was one where emotions and feelings were never acknowledged, felt or discussed, so maybe I just don't allow myself to feel anger.

About two years ago my brother came to visit and I sat him down and said "look, I have to talk to you about this." I tried to express to him what I had been going through for the previous four years and he simply couldn't take it in. I said "but don't you realise what it did to me? Don't you realise the whole way you sexualised me? You did it to me at a very early age and in circumstances where I was already fairly traumatised. I was riddled with feelings of guilt that have really fucked me up." He simply could not take it in. All he could talk about was how worried *he* had felt because he thought he was over-sexed or he was a homosexual or something like that.

He seemed totally incapable of recognising that it had had any effect on me at all. All he talked about were his own worries about himself at that time. I think it's almost certain that he was abused as a child but who by he could not say. He just knew that he had these very disturbing memories of being in a room with an old man with no clothes on.

He didn't deny what he had done to me but he didn't acknowledge it either. He told me that at the time of the abuse I had said to him one day "aren't we being homosexuals?" At that time (we're talking about the early 1950s) to be homosexual was to be unimaginably evil. It wasn't even something that you would disapprove of or maybe tolerate – it was like the worst possible thing you could possibly be.

In the end I just feel rather sorry for him. I feel in a way that he was as much a victim as I had been. Now whilst I would kill anybody who did anything like that to any of my kids, I just feel rather sad for him. I don't feel hatred for him.

At times I feel very, very grief-stricken and very sad for the child that I was because it put a major twist in my psyche. There's still sadness there. I imagine what would my life have been without this – but then your life is what it is and you become what you are through the circumstances you live with. That's just the way it is.

What did the abuse take from me?

Once more he pauses. His eyes fill with tears. It is some time before he can continue.

Innocence. Innocence and joy.

By the end of their lives I had got quite close to my parents, God bless them, and was very fond of them.

Fond? Not love?

Well, the love wasn't there to begin with and it's a long hard journey to find that love if it wasn't there at the start. They were victims of the social ambience they grew up in. I never told them of the abuse. I never told anybody. Yes, I loved them in the end.

I feel I have nothing to forgive them for because they were doing what they thought was best at the time. Or else my feelings are still so totally buried that I haven't even connected with them. Grief is the main thing when I think of the child that I was. In the early days I was an extremely happy, outgoing, imaginative and probably totally impossible child, you know. Always rushing around and making lots of noise. In many ways I had a very privileged upbringing in terms of physical circumstances, but on the other hand the emotional atmosphere was one of total absence. But the grief is healing. It just takes time.

For the future I have nothing but hope – healing, growth. I feel very good, basically. It must all sound a bit confused, to be grieving and happy. The memories are still there, and to some extent affect me every day. But with less and less force as the stress dissolves. When I think of the people with severe problems, physical handicaps and so on, I really can't complain. I think I'm one of the lucky ones. Yes, a survivor, not a victim.

ANNE

ANNE

***"I was carrying this huge load and I didn't
even know I was carrying it."***

*She is slim and athletic and radiates an aura of strength and
confidence. Her dark hair is closely cut. Now in her late
forties, she looks younger than her years. She lives alone in a
small town in the midlands.*

*She drives to Dublin with a friend to keep her company
and give her moral support. We meet in the grounds of St
Patrick's Hospital, a landmark familiar to Anne. I drive them
back to my house.*

I was precisely thirty years old when I began to develop a change in my personality. It came on almost overnight. I had a good friend at the time and she can still tell to this day when I changed. When I say I changed I began to show symptoms of what appeared to be physical illnesses, predominantly tiredness. Unbelievable tiredness for a thirty year old. I began going to various doctors and nobody could find anything wrong.

Over the next four or five years I went through every

known test. I was checked for everything from brucellosis and thyroid imbalance to possible diabetic tendencies. For several years I was in and out of hospitals for tests and I always seemed to be in hospital around the month of May – which proved later in my life to be most significant.

She lights a cigarette.

Fortunately I had a good government job and so was able to get time off, but despite this my symptoms were just getting worse and worse as I got older. I was getting more tired and exhausted as the years went by. I went to a total of fifteen different specialists during this time. Finally rheumatoid arthritis was diagnosed. I had a lot of pain and stiffness and was even wearing a collar because I couldn't turn my neck.

Finally I thought I had a reason for my symptoms. I now feel sure that those symptoms came from suppressed pain and anger. But at the time I was very pleased with the diagnosis because here at last was a reason for my terrible tiredness. Even though I was pleased to discover what was wrong, I was also very upset because I was afraid I was going to end up crippled by arthritis. However, when my doctor told me that he had previously suspected that I had Hodgkin's Disease that brought me back to my senses fairly quickly and I found it easier to accept the diagnosis.

The tiredness continued and then suddenly at about the age of forty I started having the most horrendous depressions. I was in a black hole of despair and utter hopelessness. If I had won £6 million, in the Lotto I wouldn't have been able to get up off the chair. Important things became minimal and small things became huge. I was in such turmoil, such inner pain in the head. I've never been able to find a word to describe that pain.

The depressions started coming twice a year for three months at a time. I barely functioned in my job. Then I became reclusive. I hadn't the physical energy to do anything. I gave up all the games and sport that I loved. I could hardly walk to the town which was only ten minutes away. I was carrying this huge load and I didn't even know I was carrying it. The depressions began to get worse and worse until finally a friend of mine brought me to a psychiatrist in Dublin who said I had endogenous depression. I was prescribed medication and got better and then worse again.

My huge exhaustion was still there and eventually I changed to another doctor. After three visits he twigged that things weren't right. This ordinary – well, he was really quite extraordinary – doctor realised that my problem wasn't physical, there was something more. He suggested that I should attend a psychiatrist locally. I'll never forget the diagnosis because the psychiatrist labelled me as a manic depressive. I don't know what he based his diagnosis on but I was put on a drug called Lithium which was supposed to balance my moods. Of course it balanced nothing. I just kept getting worse. I talked to him about current problems but never about my childhood.

So here I was now with another label, and I thought "well, this is my problem, I'm manic depressive." I stayed with this psychiatrist for a number of years until it got to the stage where I was depressed all the time. Then I entered a new stage that I would call just a feeling of nothingness. I went from feeling to no feeling.

I wasn't able to walk any more. I just shuffled around

like an old person along a floor. My co-ordination went. Every thing was gone. I went mentally from one state into another. I now recognise this as being the worst place I was ever in. I could hardly drive the car because I was dangerous on the road. In this state there was no pain, but it was a far more serious place to be. I wasn't feeling anything at all.

She hesitates, searching for the words to describe what happened.

I then entered from that place to a place of suicide. I later realised that I was actually arranging my own suicide. This was not going to be just an attempt – this was going to be a successful suicide. There was going to be no coming back. In work I was doing things like checking out what my next of kin would get if I died.

Eventually I had to stop work because I was no longer even able even to walk and I was only barely able to take care of myself physically. I was taking sleeping tablets. Sleep would come and go. Sometimes I would be awake all night. Sometimes I would sleep an exhausted sleep and wake up more tired than when I went to bed. But at least if I slept the night went.

I was doing nothing with my days. Absolutely nothing. I can't describe this state very well because I wasn't present in it, I was beyond feeling. I was literally just dragging myself around. I had a very good neighbour who used to come in and sit with me. I used to look straight ahead and be unable to talk. She used to just sit there. I lived in a vacuum.

It was at this time when I believe I was within a day or two of suicide that the Lord dramatically intervened in my life. That's exactly what happened. It came through a friend who used to cut my hair. She was a young girl who obviously had faith and a belief in God. Years before we had always had a great laugh and a chat, but now she saw me there just staring straight ahead. Communication had ceased for me. One day she whispered in my ear "do you ever pray?" I said "sure, what would I pray for? Who would I pray to?" She told me I could pray to God. I said "where's God? If there's a God sure I wouldn't be like this." She said that if I ever wanted to pray that I could come to her and she would help me get started.

She had whispered so gently in my ear. I can still hear that whisper. I now believe it was the Lord whispering to me.

Tears fill her eyes. We must stop for a few moments to allow her to wipe them away.

It's funny, but I can't talk about that experience anymore without crying. It was so powerful. I suppose I'm one of the lucky ones. I was able to hear that call and because I was so bad I was able to respond. If that had happened a year before I'd have laughed at her. It obviously touched some deep part of me.

The following day I went back to her and she gave me a prayer to say. It's called "The Miracle Prayer" and it goes . . .

– Lord Jesus, I come before you, just as I am. I am sorry for my sins, I repent of my sins. Please forgive me. In your name, I forgive all others for what they have done against me. I renounce Satan, the evil spirits and all their works. I give you my entire self. Lord Jesus, now and forever, I invite you into my life Jesus. I accept you as my Lord, God and Saviour. Heal

me, change me, strengthen me in body, soul and spirit. Come Lord Jesus, cover me with your precious blood, and fill me with your Holy Spirit. I love you Lord Jesus. I praise you Lord Jesus. I thank you Lord Jesus. I shall follow you every day of my life. Amen. Mary my Mother, Queen of Peace, all the Angels and Saints, please help me. Amen.

I started saying this prayer and going to Mass at lunchtime. I did it because I had nothing else. I did this for about three weeks and in the fourth week something within me began to move.

I had a friend who was a doctor and he had always taken an interest in what was wrong with me. I found myself going to him one night three weeks after starting the prayers and saying to him "will you send me to St Patrick's Hospital, if I'm ever as bad as this again?" He said to me "would you go now?"

Her voice is barely audible, as she speaks in a whisper.

I said "no, I wouldn't" because I'd had enough of doctors and specialists. He said that he had a lovely friend in the hospital that he would love me to go and see. Finally I agreed.

I went but I was so bad I had to go on a train, I couldn't drive. I was in such a state that I was barely able to walk. I remember clearly that I couldn't get off the train in the station.

The tears come again and she continues to cry quietly for a while.

I wasn't even able to get down the steps. I was afraid I'd fall and kill myself. In the big city of Dublin there were thousands of people milling all around me, it was just an awful place. I wasn't able to cross the road. I was afraid to put my foot out because the cars were whizzing by and I was there like a child stuck in the middle of the road – screaming.

Eventually I got to the other side of the road and to St Patrick's Hospital and finally the psychiatrist. I sat with him for over an hour and a half. I'll never forget it. He started asking me questions about my childhood and I told him I didn't remember my childhood. He said "you don't remember anything about being a child?" and I said no. Finally he said "Anne, something happened you in your childhood, something happened in those years you can't remember. Things will never come right for you until we look in and see what's there." He told me that he had a lovely therapist that he would send me to and that he would phone me in two days. He phoned me in two days with her name and asked me to come up and see her.

This all happened within five weeks after my young friend had mentioned the Lord to me. I now had a psychiatrist and a therapist. That was the start.

She asks if we can stop as she needs to draw breath for a while.

I can remember innocently asking my therapist the first day I arrived "how long will I be here?" and she said a couple of months. She produced some sheets of paper and asked me to write about different parts of my life. What I remembered up to five years of age and then from five to ten and from ten to fifteen years. I sat there blankly looking at these sheets of paper.

I had one memory only, and that memory was of a man abusing me. I remembered one episode of this man having sex with me, and that's really all I had of my childhood. That was all I had to go on. Luckily I had that memory because that was how we got into all the rest.

In my own experience of dealing with repressed memory it's as if an outline comes first. It's like circles. Like a dart-board. The outer circle of memories is where you're remembering that things weren't right. My therapist suggested that I go back to the house of my childhood and talk to a neighbour, a local woman who remembered me as a child. This woman gave me a head start.

I had been left with the impression, or I gave myself the impression, that I had a wonderful childhood. If I met you ten years ago and you had asked me what kind of childhood I'd had, I would have said "oh God, I was privileged, I was treated like a piece of Waterford glass." I created that for myself and it was very hard to break that image.

So I went to see my old neighbour because I had no other way of getting any information. She would have known my family very well. She wasn't a huge friend, but a neighbour and an observer as well. She very quickly broke the picture that I had been left with. She said that the neighbours used to say "poor Anne". This was a huge thing for me to hear. When I asked her why did they say that she said "your mother used to take your brothers to school and she'd go on and you used to be left running along on your own, trailing behind with your school bag."

I also remembered an aunt of mine would say to me

when I was older "I used to think there was something wrong with you when you were a baby. Because when I'd look into your pram I got no reaction whatsoever from you." My aunt had tried to get me to smile or respond but she said I was a blank. As an infant I used to just stare at the top of the pram with no reactions.

This memory of my aunt coupled with what my neighbour had told me was very hard for me to hear. It was a huge thing for me to realise that the neighbours were feeling sorry for me. My neighbour mentioned a few other things that left her with the knowledge that things were not any way right in my house. The locals knew that this man used to come and take me off when I was about four or five. I remembered the man coming but I didn't know that it went back that far. This was the man who used to abuse me. But my memory had been that I was twelve or thirteen when he abused me, and here was this woman telling me that it went on from the time I was four.

The man was a friend of my mothers. I believe she produced him for no other reason than to protect her own carry-on. I would say she had him to protect herself. If anything ever came out he would be blamed. All the neighbours knew that he was bringing me out for walks and off on his bicycle. When we went out he used to abuse me.

I went back to my therapist with all this information and she later described me at that stage as being like a balloon and she was just holding a pin to it. I was either going to kill myself or I was going to come up with the story. It was just ready to come out.

It came very soon, slowly and painfully, but it came. There was a sort of outer layer, first of memories of this man and him coming into the house. Remembering things is only the outer layer. You have to get into the inner layer to relive the thing itself as a child and release your pain. You could stay on the outside layer all your life, but until you get into the inside you can never heal yourself properly. You've got to relive the pain that you couldn't let out at the time. At the time the thing is happening it is so painful that you sort of opt out of your body. You have to get back into your body and release the pain. The first year or two of therapy was all this outline stuff. I had to relive his abuse and I thought that's all there was.

It's very hard to describe this, but then a second layer came and this was around my mother. It didn't come in memories first, it came in feelings. When the first of these memories came up a very good friend, who I had met at a prayer group, was with me. I believe I was led by the Lord to people who could help me and keep me safe on this journey. This friend was there for the first nights when I found myself hiding behind the couch from my mother. My mother was coming to get us.

I was over forty, but it was as if I was only four or five years old. I would hide behind the couch and make my friend hide with me. I'd even throw a rug over our heads because I was so afraid that my mother was going to get us. My friend would say "what is it?" and I'd say "she's coming to get us." So all these feelings around my mother came first and I knew that something had happened with her. These kind of memories went on for ages.

During this I was in a most horrendous state. Before these memories came I would get the most appalling headaches.

She cradles her head.

My therapist would be stirring stuff when I was talking to her. When I came away from her little things would begin to rise, but they rose through blinding, pumping headaches. Then I'd ring my friend and she would arrive and I'd then become the child and tell her what was going on. I would play the game with her and she would become my friend, my adult protector and I would tell her what my mother was doing. It had started with a fear around my mother and a knowledge within me that my mother had destroyed me in some way.

One of the first flashbacks I had was in Glendalough, County Wicklow. I was with another friend in a bus full of people and this tremendous headache came and the exhaustion with it. I had to get away from the crowd. Luckily my friend followed to see what was wrong. I began to get all hot and bothered trying to breathe and I remembered my mother holding a pillow over my face and nose trying to smother me. I relived that gasping for breath while sitting on the wall down in Glendalough. I was physically gasping, physically reliving the actual incident and pushing with my hands trying to push this pillow away. I was probably four or five when this incident happened. That was my first full concrete memory.

She had tried to smother me with a pillow on hundreds of occasions. Once she almost succeeded, because I remember her being out on the road screaming that I was dead. She was telling the yarn to somebody of what happened, but I knew that she had tried to kill me. But I survived. That was when she went a step too far and almost succeeded. I believe she would have killed me if she ever thought she would have got away with it.

I think it's important at this stage to point out that this wasn't a straightforward case of sexual abuse. This was a story of torture. I would say my mother was really trying to destroy me, to kill me. But she wasn't able to fully do it because she was afraid of being caught. It wasn't a case of abuse for sexual gratification. It was a constant attempt to destroy me, her daughter, in the most violent ways. I later realised that as her daughter I was obviously a constant reminder to her of her own past.

I remembered periods of being put into my room. I spent most of my young life in that room, my bedroom. I'd be put in the room with my dog for company. The dog would just arrive and I'd let it in and I know sometimes my older brother would come along and take the dog off on me. It was like taking my right arm when he'd take the dog out of the room, because it was my companion.

To make it even worse this was the room I shared with my mother. I had to sleep with her as well. Then I relived being hungry and that was a huge issue. I had memory flashbacks of being locked in that room most of the time when I came home from school and not given my dinner or tea. I was often made to sit and watch my brothers eat while I was given no food. I was starved on a number of occasions and I can tell you that hunger was one of the worst pains. When these memories surfaced in therapy I developed huge problems around food. I had to have food or I'd start getting weak and feel I was going to die.

I was always told that everything that happened to me was because I was so bold. I was constantly told I was bold, but I could never tell you what I did that made me bold. So I had an awful problem as a child wondering how I could be good, because I didn't know how you could be good.

You might ask where my father was in all this. He was working and this was all done behind his back. You might think this was very odd, but it happened. My father was just a doormat in the house. It's very easy for a parent to control a child and a partner and have one not knowing what the other is doing. It sounds weird but it was done. The only thing that kept me going as a child was knowing that my father loved me. He never told me but I knew innately. That was probably what kept me going through the horrors of what was happening at home.

Then I had more memory flashbacks of her raping me with lots of things – hairbrushes, candles you name it. Anything she could lay her hands on she would stick up through me. This is what I mean when I say that it wasn't subtle because it was violence. At the time it must have been terribly painful but I held the pain and I've only let it out in the last five years. That's what I mean by going into the pain and reliving the incident and letting out the pain that you couldn't let out at the time.

She must have started this before I could even talk. All I know is that my aunt felt there was something wrong with me as a baby. So she was up to something at that stage as well. When I came into knowledge at about the age of three or four this was going on constantly. It went on all the way through my childhood – repetition after repetition.

Again we must stop for a few minutes. She stands up to walk around the room, pausing at the window to look out at the garden as if to gather her strength for what is still to come.

I've remembered other things that she did. I was burned with matches for no reason. Something would have happened to put her in bad form. I don't know if I caused it or something else did. I was told everything was my fault anyway so I never knew what caused her anger. She burned my genitals with matches. She broke my teeth. I have had four false teeth since I was a youngster. I remember when she was washing my hair in one of those old enamel sinks she caught my head and thumped my face off it breaking my teeth.

She slaps one hand onto the other.

She held my hand over naked flames on the gas cookers. These were regular things that she did from when I was about the age of three or four up to eleven or twelve. Then things changed at that time.

During this time also the man was taking me off and abusing me. It must have been with her collusion, because who would let their four-year-old off with a man up and down the road for an hour every evening at four o'clock on the cross-bar of his bicycle? When I was talking to my neighbour about him she remembered that he didn't have a good reputation. So it would look to me that my mother was very cold and calculating as well as being so broken herself. She obviously worked out that in order to protect herself if anything ever happened she could produce this man and he would be blamed. That's the only reason I can give you.

My neighbour did say that people suspected things were going on, but nobody ever did anything. People refused to believe that such things happened and still do. People feel helpless. I later had to deal with my anger towards people for not interfering, for not helping.

The anger can still be heard in her voice.

My mother went to Mass regularly and she used to send us children out to eight o'clock Mass every morning. I can remember I always hated wind and still do. I used to be on my bicycle trying to cycle against the wind. I couldn't sit on the saddle because I was all swollen. I can describe my genitalia as being constantly black and blue, red and bleeding. I used to struggle up and down the road to Mass. To this day I can't tolerate wind because of that effort of cycling against it.

We didn't have a bathroom when I was a child but we had an old tin bath. My older brother got everything first. I got second best in everything. So he got the cleanest water. Then when he was out it was my turn. She used to pour boiling water from the kettle into the bath but not on top of my body. Because if it was on my body it would be seen. I used to have to pull my feet up tight to my body to escape the boiling water. She did everything she could to inflict injury and pain.

At that stage my brothers didn't know what was going on. She did it when they were outside playing, I was never let out to play or mix with people. If I had a friend as a child they weren't let inside our door. I wasn't let go to other children's houses to play or stay the night. I was never allowed to go anywhere.

Everything was done to protect the secret. Nowadays these things would be more obvious.

I was sent to a school which was much further away than the nearest school. I thought it was for reasons of grandeur because it was a school for the professional children at the time and my father wasn't a professional. Primary school was totally and utterly controlled by my mother. She would meet me at the gate whenever school was over and I would be marched or cycled home. But it was a nice school and there was no violence in it. So I was protected there. In the other school, nearer home, the regime was somewhat tougher. So school was a reprieve during the day.

At that time doctors and nurses used to go around the schools to examine children for various medical problems but I was always kept at home on those days. My mother would know the nurse was coming and I'd be brought home. The nurse wasn't let look at me anywhere. Whenever I needed a doctor my mother always brought me to her own doctor. My injuries were always to areas that couldn't be seen, mainly to my private parts which were constantly sore and swollen. The broken tooth couldn't be hidden but she had a story for that. Of course smothering me with a pillow left no mark.

I presume she also came up with a reason why my hand was burned. She probably told my father that I burned it on the fire. A four-year-old doesn't say "that's a lie." I'd been warned that I would be killed if I told.

The man who was abusing me told me that if I told my mother or anyone else what he was doing he would kill my mother. So how could a small child growing up like that tell anybody anything? I never said anything to my father because I was terrorised by the threats and of course, everything was my fault.

I slept in the same bed as my mother because she didn't sleep with my father. That was the only bed I knew. I could never go to sleep properly because I always had to be on my guard. I couldn't trust her for two minutes because I never knew when I was going to be under attack. I used to sleep at the bottom of the bed, trying to hide under the covers. So I spent a lot of my life at the bottom of that bed trying to get away from her. I was constantly alert because I never knew what would happen next. All my young childhood I always had a problem with sleeping.

The only happiness I had in my childhood was when we used to go on holiday to the seaside for two weeks every year. I still gravitate to the sea all the time. It was the only happiness I knew because I used to share a room with my brothers. My mother and father must have shared a bed on holidays, because they probably had to in front of people.

I had my father all to myself and those were the happiest times in my life – two weeks every year. My father was present all the time. He wasn't working and I wasn't in the bed with my mother so I was perfectly safe. I had my father to myself all day, and so did my brothers, he was there to protect me. I used to be in a terrible state a few days before we went home because I knew it would all start again when we returned.

Once more her voice is barely a whisper.

She never showed any remorse or said she was sorry. The only time she ever hugged me, and this is horrible to talk about as well, was after what I had to do at night – sexually please my mother. I was trained in the art of oral sex from the age of four. The only time I ever found a hug was after that. The only time I ever felt love in my life from her was when I obliged her in this way. I think she used to put her arm around me afterwards. That was all I knew. It happened constantly. I don't know whether it was all night, or every night or once a week, but it was on a regular basis.

Her voice is an angry whisper.

These memories came in layers and I thought I had remembered the worst. They come in intensity and sometimes the worst ones come later than the others. They come when you're able for them, able to take them. Only in the last year have I remembered what happened with my older brother. When he was about twelve and I was eleven, I remembered an incident where she forced him to have sex with me. He was in the most horrendous state at the time, but she forced him and she continued to do so for the next number of years. I had no protection because she was present for most of this or in another room knowing this was going on. She would send my brother to do it and eventually he developed a liking for it. So he did it on his own.

At around this time my mother got sick with cancer and was in and out of hospital. When she was in hospital I was still never safe in the house because he was doing this. So I still couldn't sleep because I had to keep my eye on him. I used to hide but he would pull me out from under the bed. I used to pull a dressing table across in front of the door so as I would hear him coming, but I was never able to sleep peacefully.

I never screamed because I had been warned. That was the awful side of it. He did it when my father was working. Or after school when my mother was there or when she was in hospital. My father would have come to my defence, but it wasn't done when he was there, everything was done when he wasn't in the house. My brother continued doing this and it ended up that I became pregnant at the age of fourteen.

She says that she needs another break now. After some minutes we continue.

It's hard to believe in my innocence that I didn't know anything at that stage about babies or about how you became pregnant. I was one of the most ignorant fourteen-year-olds there ever was. But at that time lots of fourteen-year-olds were as ignorant as I was. We're talking about over thirty years ago. So I was packed off to a boarding school, or so I was told.

When I got there I remember that there were no lessons or study. There were nuns and there were a lot of women, older women. I don't know now how old they were. When I was fourteen a twenty-year-old would probably have looked ancient to me. They were obviously teenage girls and probably girls in their twenties and thirties. To me they all appeared way older than me. I was the youngest there. I was given into the care of one of these young women. Her name was Eileen.

When I was in this boarding school I was gradually getting bigger and fatter. In my ignorance and innocence I had no idea why this was happening. What I had been through up until now was bad but this was the worst experience of all. I now realise that what I thought was a boarding school was in fact a mother and baby home. The home itself seemed to be a nice place. They were kind people. I was well treated, well-fed and well looked after. There was no cruelty there. The cruelty was in the fact that I was ignorant as to why I was there. I didn't know why the other women were there either.

I didn't know it then but I know now that the babies were born on the premises. My room upstairs was very close to where the babies were born. The real terror for me was that I would be awoken by women screaming in the night. Obviously this didn't happen every night but when it did I presumed they were being killed. The next morning the women were gone, so I was sure something terrible had happened to them.

Eileen, the young woman who was looking after me, was fabulous but she had clearly been forbidden to tell me what I was doing there. She went on with the pretence that I was getting big because we were eating too much. I developed a form of bulimia because I thought if I could get this food up out of me then I mightn't get fat.

Eileen was gorgeous. I'd love to meet her today and I may even search for her yet. In her own way she was able to prepare me for the fact that she would be leaving soon. Her baby and mine were obviously due at around the same time. She was a very kind-hearted person and I have a lot to thank her for, because without her there I would have gone crazy. No baby was ever mentioned but she was able to prepare me for the day when she would no longer be with me. That was a huge blessing. She said "I'll be going soon and when that happens you'll be coming after me. You'll be next and we'll be going home then." So I knew I'd be going home yet I was confused about being killed.

She cries again, sobbing as she talks of Eileen.

She was small, with black curly hair, and was constantly smiling. We were always having fun together. I remember I used to fold sheets in a laundry and she used to be there with me and she was always happy and smiling. I don't remember spending a lot of time with anyone other than her. I was terrified in that place but in the blackness of it all she was the saving grace for me. I'd love to meet her now to thank her for what she did and for the preparation she gave me. When I woke up one morning she was gone.

Then my turn for the screaming came.

I remember being tied to the bed and thinking I was going to be killed. I must at one stage have pleaded for my life because a woman who was at my right hand side said to me "it's a baby, it's okay, it's only a baby." I think she was some kind of mid-wife and at that stage the fear seemed to recede. I don't remember a lot about the labour but I do remember all my pain was in my back. The next thing I remember was that I heard a baby crying as they brought it out the door and then I knew it was a baby. I don't know whether it was a boy or a girl or whether it's alive or dead. I never saw the baby since.

Her voice is again a whisper.

After the baby was born I woke up the next day in another building with a certain amount of relief about me – I know that. I think I was relieved that I was alive. Then they were trying to make me eat and I'd eat and then vomit it up again. I thought it was eating that had given me that lump so I wasn't going to get heavy and get this lump again.

Then the most surprising thing happened. Out of such awfulness, suffering and pain came the maternal instinct. Even at fourteen years of age and after such trauma it clicked in instantly. When I was in this new building I used to get up every night and go around the place to see if I could find the baby. I would look in all the windows at the back, trying to find my baby.

Weeping she continues in a low voice.

I can understand the instinct of a mother, I found that overpowering. The feeling of a mother was still there, even though the mother didn't know how she got the baby.

I don't know what they did with the babies. Mine was gone straightaway. I don't remember seeing babies, but that doesn't mean that they weren't there. I think some of those babies might have gone to America. Mine could have been adopted straight away. I've no idea what the story is, but I intend to find out when I'm ready.

During all the time I was there nobody came to visit me. I used to spend Sundays sitting outside waiting for someone to come and bring me home. Nobody ever came. But eventually they came. A few days after the baby was born my mother came and brought me home.

She did all these things herself. I don't know where my father thought I was gone.

When I came home then I became a different person because I had suffered so much. I turned against my father and everybody else. I just instantly dismissed them all as I didn't believe my father cared any more. I didn't give a shit about him because as far as I was aware he had allowed me to go through all this. So I just clicked into being a whole new person. That is obviously when I split. I just left it all there and put on this whole new front – I became a new person and didn't care about my family any more. I was fifteen at this stage and I had reached my limit of suffering.

My brother started his activities again when I came home but my mother tried to stop him this time – and succeeded. Although it did happen a few times after I came home, because he had found a new way of doing it, which was oral sex. But I became very physically strong. I never was physically strong before but energy came from nowhere to protect myself. I developed a kind of "warrior strength" and I had a sense of knowing what had caused the baby. Now I was fighting for my life and I got strength from places I never knew were there. In the end he wasn't really able for me any more. I was able for him.

My mother's cancer had worsened at this stage and there were a couple of years when she would be missing from the house for periods of time while she was in hospital. Part of me would want her dead and part of me would want her back. She was dying and going back and forth between hospital and home. She finally died in her late forties. I was sixteen.

When she died I had such mixed emotions. I

honestly don't know what I felt. I was devastated at the time, but one part of me was very pleased that she was gone. She had always threatened to leave me. Even when she was sick she told me everything was my fault and that she had never been well since the day I was born. It took me until six years ago to sort out the fact that I wasn't responsible for killing her. If I had been younger when she died I would have been totally traumatised by her death. But I wasn't, I was only sort of half-traumatised.

My elder brother left home at this stage to study and myself and my father were left.

My younger brother was in boarding school. It was fine, but the adoration I'd had for my father had changed because of the baby. I think I figured somewhere in my mind that he must have known where I was and did nothing to help me.

I don't know where my father fits into all this. Everybody asks that question and I don't know the answer. I only know that my father would never have witnessed such suffering for me and stood by. I believe that. I don't know what happened over the baby or where was he at the time, I've no idea what he was told. I assumed in my mind that he knew. I felt this because all my life afterwards if a friend of mine came to the house and my father would be telling stories about me as a child – funny stories or whatever – I would never once hear him say "do you remember the time you went to the boarding school?" I never heard that word mentioned again in our house. I lost all association with my father then. I broke this love bond I had with him, and we had a kind of stormy relationship in the house when my mother was gone.

My elder brother kept coming back on holidays but by then I had buried all memories of the abuse. Two years after the birth of the baby all the memories were gone. It was only when my brother was coming home that fear rose in me. I was always afraid of my brother, but I could never tell you why. He would arouse some terror in me.

I developed a rebellious streak and left school before I did my Leaving Certificate. If it happened today I would probably be into drugs and alcohol. There wasn't a lot of harm to get into in those days but I got into all the harm you could get into. Innocent harm. I learned to smoke, to drink and all the things you learn at that age.

I ran around all the time. I was constantly on the go, constantly running. Up until the time I was very sick with depression I couldn't sit on my own for five minutes. I couldn't be on my own so I was always in the middle of people everywhere and anywhere, playing sports and into amateur dramatics and all sorts of things. I was never at home for five minutes. Strangely enough I always lived at home with my father.

Some years later I came home one day and my father was dead on the kitchen floor. This was before the worst of the depressions came. When he died I plummeted downhill very quickly. The hospital visits for physical ailments came before my father's death and the depressions came after it.

He had never made any reference to anything my mother ever did to me and he never talked about her. I was aware of my older brother's feelings for my mother. He hated her. My father and my brother were aware of my concocted feelings for my mother – that she was like the Virgin Mary, a most beautiful mother. So how could they talk to me about my mother? They were aware of the reality of this woman, but probably not what she did to me. I feel sure that my brother fully repressed his part in my abuse.

In therapy one day my mother's death came up and I said "she left." All my young life my mother had threatened to leave me because I was so bold and when she died a side of me believed that she had finally carried out her threat. The therapist said to me "your mother didn't leave you. Your mother died." She told me that she wanted me to go and stand at her grave. She said "I want you to realise that your mother is down there. She's not gone somewhere, she's dead in that grave. Even though you witnessed the funeral – the reality hasn't hit you."

I went and stood at her grave and when I went back I phoned my therapist. I shouted down the phone "she didn't leave me. She died." I can't understand the psychological thing of all that, but that's what happened. It was like a sack of potatoes had been lifted off my shoulders "she didn't leave me. She died."

Before I started to feel unwell people would have thought I was a great character altogether. I was great gas, I was great fun and full of the joys of life. When I started to feel unwell, people would notice there were two sides to me. They used to say to me "which Anne have I now?" I could be five different Annes. So I would probably have had something like a multiple personality disorder.

Lots of people who have suffered like this would have become very violent or alcoholic. They could have turned to drug addiction or prostitution or become neurotic. Of course I was neurotic, but I was fortunate that I never became any of those other things. I turned it all inwards and it ate me away in lumps inside. I was so angry, but not obviously angry, it was all inside me rotting away.

I was a perfectionist. I was always putting on a show for people. It was as if I was on stage all my life. I was a great comedian and loved acting. People used to seek my company when I was in good form for the laugh they would have. I've often heard it said that comedians are sometimes those who live closest to despair. I couldn't be funny for you now if I tried. I wouldn't be able.

My picture of myself was that I literally looked like a monster and that people were talking about me every time I passed by. I thought they were remarking on how ugly I was and short and fat. My own image of myself was in shit. If I was a friend of yours twenty years ago and we went into a pub you'd have to get up to the bar. I wouldn't. I'd give you all the money in the world but I wouldn't stand up because everyone would be looking at me and thinking how horrible and ugly I was.

Despite this I had lots of boyfriends. But it was safe to have boyfriends then because there were no sexual demands put on you in those days. But the minute anyone ever got too close I was gone to the next boy. It was like that with friends too. When a friendship became too close, I'd run to the next friend. I had a problem with intimacy, any kind of intimacy, even that of friendship. I would develop a friendship to a certain level and then I was gone. I developed the boyfriends in the same way. So I turned off a switch and instead of becoming a sexaholic I became an asexual being.

I wasn't tuned in to my feelings. I wasn't aware on

any level of how I operated but I was very much aware of my image of myself and how awful it was. I envied every body else. I thought every body else had it and I had nothing. Everybody seemed to have a large happy family and had relatives to visit on Sunday and have dinner with them. I had nobody to do that with. I don't envy other people anymore, because now I see that most people have problems. I thought every one was living the perfect life and that I was just existing.

At work I was also badly bullied by a boss at one stage. Others were able to tell him to go to hell but he honed in on me. Today I would be far better able to stick up for myself and protect myself. But then I wasn't. I feel that until the healing process started there was something like a stamp on my forehead saying "abuse me please." There is something recognisable about somebody who is bullied or abused. It's as if you're open for more abuse. There's also a more subtle thing going on – you become comfortable with being bullied and abused because it's all you know. It's very hard to cease being a victim.

The healing has come for me slowly and in layers. The last bit of memory about the baby was the worst. What I have remembered in the last year has changed my life totally. But I now have the feeling "I don't have to run anymore." Now it's like the last piece of the jigsaw is in place. I don't have to pretend anything anymore. The running is over. There's more peace inside but there are still issues to be dealt with.

When I am stronger I want to find out do I have a thirty-three-year old daughter or son somewhere, and, if so, where? What blocks and closed doors will I come up against? I suppose I'll never be complete until I find this child, or find where it went.

She weeps for a few moments for her lost child.

Why did my mother do what she did? Well I don't believe that you could be born into any sort of normality and do something like that. Looking back on my mother's family, this was a repeated pattern. All the men in her family were depressives and the women as well as being depressive were also quite disturbed. Some of them were in marriages that didn't last and they were having affairs. All of the things that you didn't do at that time. These are common things today, but they weren't then. They were all sick and had psychosomatic symptoms of every kind of disease.

So the pattern was there. I believe when my mother had a daughter the recreation of herself had arrived and she couldn't look at me. I see that she tried to destroy this daughter. I believe if she could have got away with killing me at birth or later she probably would have done so. I would say I brought up all her own pain and suffering. I believe that even getting my brother involved in this was learned behaviour. I don't think any mother would invent something like that for no reason. She tried to destroy me.

She took my life from me. Sometimes I could argue that it might have been better had she killed me at the time, because murder is murder and I'd have been saved all the suffering. But incest is a different kind of murder. It's murder of the person, murder of the soul, murder of the heart. She took everything from me. She destroyed my life, my brothers' lives and my father's life. She destroyed her own life. I was just an innocent victim of her destruction.

My feelings about her now change from time to time. But overall I don't bear her any ill will. She's dead for a number of years. I hope she's at rest somewhere because I believe that she suffered herself . . .

Anne cries quietly during the next few minutes.

. . . and that she didn't get the chance that I got to be healed. I believe that she came to me from her own suffering and I also believe that I was the luckier of the two of us because I got a chance to heal. She died in her pain and in her agony.

Having said that, I had to go through all of the anger in the process of therapy. I beat her off walls and ditches and all sorts of things to get up my anger, which was a healthy thing to do. You're entitled to these emotions. You're only fooling yourself if you think you can forgive without dealing with the anger. Anger inside is destructive and unhealthy in every way. I feel that if you stay in an unforgiving and angry place then you remain a prisoner. I've been a prisoner for too long. I don't need to be a prisoner any more. I believe that the time must come for us to forgive and that's not something you can force on people, it's something people must arrive at. To leave it behind I think that you must come to a place of forgiveness to have a chance of freedom. I believe I was given the grace by God to forgive her when the time was right, because I don't think humanly I could have done so. Now I just hope she's at rest.

What I've gained most from all of this is an

experience of the Lord's love for me. I experienced that very powerfully at a time when I was about to kill myself and I experienced it very powerfully in the early days of my healing when I was overcome with a feeling of love and peace. I don't know why it happened for me. I wouldn't be here to tell this story without the experience I had of His love for me and His presence. Life to me today is about my spiritual life.

The Lord put people in my way to accompany me on this journey. I felt I was being led by the hand to those who could help and support me through this time. Words can never express the gratitude I feel to those friends who kept me going from day to day. I had a friend who I used to go to when all the memories were coming up and she would pray with me for the Lord to take away the fear.

I would go home and the memory would come up quite simply on a lot of occasions. Often the fear of what's coming is actually worse than the thing that comes. Fortunately I had a good friend with whom I shared a house during those years. She was able to accompany me as I actively relived the memory of each incident. There was also a couple whom I visited weekly who provided a safe place in their home for prayer, sharing and friendship. All of these were essential in my healing. I realise that my experience of the Lord doesn't happen for everybody and I don't know why it happened for me.

It was as if a whole structure of support was being set up. Without my therapist I don't know where all this would have ended. She offered me the great gift of being accepted unconditionally and loved and encouraged through it all.

I'm very aware that I'm not part of that world I used to be in – the world of running. I've stopped living in that world and I have found the peace that we all search for. We find it for a time and it goes and we find it again. It's the peace of Christ within. I never knew what peace was. Today I know what it is and it's the difference between night and day. In a way I have been blessed to have suffered so much because I've found the important thing. My suffering left me open to the Lord and able to accept Him. I can live in peace knowing how much I'm loved by the Lord. Without that I'd have nothing. I would be as vulnerable as I ever was without that. Peace brings acceptance.

Again Anne says that we must stop so that she can gather her thoughts.

It would be foolish to say that I feel at peace every day. It's as if years ago my whole body was burnt from head to toe and covered in raw red wounds. Now they're gone into a scar on my skin and if you look you'll see the mark of that burn and I will always carry that mark. But this load is out of me now and it's a much easier load to carry now that it's uncovered. When you know the cause of all your pain it makes it so much easier.

MICHAELA

MICHAELA

"Entering the convent removed the burden of sexuality from me."

Michaela is small, dark-haired and vivacious. Academically gifted and with a beautiful singing voice, she left school at eighteen and entered a convent. Now in her mid-forties she is still a nun but lives separately from her community in a neat, sun-filled apartment. Dressed in a warm pink sweater and tan slacks she wears a profusion of silver jewellery; a silver sun earring dangles from one ear and a silver moon from the other.

By the time I was in my thirties I was principal of a large girls' school. People in authority and others had a real sense of security in me. I was unflappable, I didn't know fear, I was calmness personified. No matter what I had to do I did it without getting fussed at all. I ran a school and was considered a good principal. That was wonderful and I got great satisfaction out of that affirmation. In the course of my life I had learned to do the right thing and have the right ideas. I was always admired.

I believed in a loving God and I felt that although my childhood had been difficult I was lucky. My mother had died when I was a baby. I remember knowing somebody else, who had been depressed for years, whose mother had also died when she was small. I remember thinking "aren't I so lucky that it hasn't affected me in the same way." I felt that this was God's blessing. I had good friends and was very popular but God was always the one who had been constant and faithful to me when things weren't great.

I had been a nun for about fifteen years when I went to Africa for awhile. It was a time of renewal and I took time off from school to go. For various reasons the timing of my trip wasn't great. In Africa I became extremely lonely, which I'd never been really aware of before. I became very aware of family and of my mother in a way I'd never been before. The memory of her death when I was a baby began sparking things off in me.

During that Lent I had this feeling that I should go to the desert, so I went there on retreat. I went with the idealistic notion of meeting God alone, without props. Before I went I had begun to get quite frightened about going. It was very hot and I'd heard things that made me uneasy and I thought maybe it wasn't such a good idea after all. But there was a priest there that somebody knew and he was going to be near enough to me. He felt it was fairly safe. I knew I would have a lot of time on my own and I wanted that time alone.

I wasn't aware of feeling awful in the desert, it was quite OK. Then when I was coming out of the desert I saw a man drowning. Usually people drive through the empty wadis of the rivers but there was a flash flood, because there had been heavy rain in the mountains and it had flowed in torrents through the desert. We had to wait until the rains went down before we could cross. An African man had got impatient, took some drink, and drove through the river. There was a makeshift bridge but we actually watched him being sucked in by the river. He wasn't far away. A most awful feeling of helplessness and guilt hit me. I felt helpless because I was very near the man and couldn't save him and then guilt because neither I nor anybody else had done anything. Nobody had helped because these rivers were so dangerous. When the river began to go down a bit, about four hours later, men went in but of course he was dead.

The next morning when I passed through the river something in my chest went. I knew something had cracked inside me.

I was met outside the desert by a nun and we went to her community. There were carpets on the floor and paint on the wall. In the desert the place I stayed in had been purely functional. There was no paint on the wall and just a bed in the room, but I hadn't noticed because of the sunshine. When I saw the feminine touches in the community I just cried and cried.

I also saw people dressed in clothes. That was an awful shock after the desert. I understood what "culture shock" meant for the first time. In the desert the women wore sheets around their waists or if they were very far out in the bush they wore a goatskin from the waist down. They were topless – beautiful women. The men had been given blankets, traditionally by the British, so they threw the blanket over their shoulders and it covered some of them. There was a real dignity about them.

One of the big things about my experience in Africa was that I realised that these people had a dignity in their semi-nakedness. Yet the children were being made to wear uniforms in schools, which became torn. The adults were starting to wear nylon European clothes. Can you imagine the discomfort of nylon clothes in desert heat? I felt so awful that we had taken away their culture and dignity in so many ways.

Her voice shakes with emotion.

If they went to Mass most of them couldn't go to Communion because, although we brought them the so called "good news", we also told them they couldn't go to Communion because their lifestyle wasn't Christian. Many of the women were second or third wives and, most of the men had a number of wives.

The children could go to Communion but once they became thirteen or fourteen that became a problem because they were beginning to be sorted out into relationships. I had a real problem with that and I began to realise that so much of the trappings of Christianity were European and had nothing to do with love and with bringing "good news" to anybody. So again I began to feel guilty and helpless about that and the fact that I had bought into these ideas. With the feeling of helplessness an utter depression descended on me.

After six months in Africa I came back to Ireland. I was totally immobilised psychologically. I had to go back into my job, or I thought I did. I hadn't the energy to try to get out of it. I was in a severe depression but didn't know it. I was very confused. I didn't care about anything and I didn't care about the school. I tried to run it as best I could but I really hadn't the energy.

I don't know whether anybody noticed anything was wrong with me or not – I think they thought I would be fine. They were concerned about me, all right, but I suppose they thought that I would gradually recover. I think they also felt it wouldn't be good for me to be taken out of the school.

I became totally immobilised and knew that I couldn't live in the state I was in. I couldn't live at the rate I was living. I realised I was badly in need of help and so I chose to go to a psychiatrist and started seeing him regularly. God was gone from my life, anything I'd ever believed in was gone. I would have stayed in bed all day if I could. It was suggested that I should become involved in activity because it wouldn't be good for me to stay in bed.

I was exhausted because I had been overworking for years. I had been a workaholic of major proportions, I would do everything and then I hadn't time to think about myself. I was running away. I was in a very bad way, extremely upset, full of despair and suicidal. I'd say if I'd been pushed hard enough and if people hadn't listened to me I would have committed suicide. I had sleeping tablets so it wouldn't have been be too hard.

She weeps quietly for some moments.

Yet there was something in me that held on. But I

thought a lot about committing suicide. If I had had the courage to end it I would have. I just wanted to be dead, I envied the old, they didn't have to think about the future. The future was death and I thought that would be great – just get me out of this pain.

I felt so dreadful that I felt that I was nearly a danger to be with. I was contaminated. No wonder God had abandoned me. I felt that other people had liked me because I had performed and been a nice person. I didn't feel I was a nice person any longer and they would see through me. Therefore I felt that any friends I had before wouldn't be friends any more. I didn't know what I was doing in religious life and I certainly felt that if the sisters knew about me I could be thrown out.

She cries quietly throughout this.

During that time I started to remember that as a teenager I had been very disturbed, and I didn't know why. I found the teenage years very hard and I was very, very sad during them, even though I had been very outgoing as a child. When I was preparing for Confirmation I remember being told the story of Saint Maria Goretti. The version I was given was that she had died rather than let a man touch her. That put me into an absolute spin of horror. There was the feeling that God considered it was better to be murdered than to be touched by a man. To allow a man to go near you meant that it was the woman's fault. Any version of sex I ever heard was that it was the woman's fault if a man got aroused – she had behaved improperly and she was to blame. Maria Goretti was canonised because she was so wonderful to die rather than sully her purity.

Around that time I also discovered that my mother had died when I was a baby, I hadn't known until then. I had been brought up to understand that my stepmother was my mother. But I always felt there was something strange and I was always trying to get information. I had vague memories that I couldn't place together. Nobody had told me about my mother's death. I was eleven or twelve before I found out.

I think the combination of those two things filled me with an awful sense of guilt. The Maria Goretti story resulted in me putting a huge mask on my face because if people really knew me I would be considered fit for murder or condemned. I had a memory of having had sexual activity with a boy, a distant relative, from the age of four to the age of eleven. That memory was very clear always – but I hadn't a sense of feeling guilty about it until I heard the Maria Goretti story. Then I discovered that there was something very seriously wrong with what I had been doing and I hadn't known. The boy had been giving me attention. I liked the attention and didn't see anything wrong with it. He wasn't that much older than I was. At the time I thought he was a lot older, but now I realise he can have only been a few years older than me.

My parents didn't know about this. I don't know where they were, but they weren't in the house. He used to arrive up when he'd see my parents go out. I used to be afraid at night when I was on my own and so he was company – and that's the way it began. I think it only stopped when I heard the Maria Goretti story. My periods had begun so I was afraid of becoming pregnant. It was all very vague because I didn't have any kind of sex education. But I said I didn't want it any more. Then he said "I thought you were enjoying yourself." So I said "no, I don't want it any more" and he stopped.

The fact that he stopped nearly made it worse – it must definitely have been my fault. Somehow I must have been encouraging him and I could have stopped it long before or it might never have happened at all. I had allowed this boy to do what he did and I was responsible. It was a sexual relationship that I was responsible for – it wasn't abuse in my mind. When I was thinking of entering the convent at sixteen or seventeen I went to confession and told the priest. He said "as long as you didn't have pleasure, it was okay."

I found out about my mother because I used to root through drawers and papers looking for information. I remember seeing the date on my parents' marriage certificate. They had been married after I was born. So I asked if I was an orphan and was told I wasn't and that the date in the marriage certificate was a misprint. I continued rooting and then I remember seeing something else with the same date and I realised that it wasn't a misprint at all. So I went back to Mammy and asked if I was an orphan and she said to wait until Daddy came in. So Daddy explained that Mammy (my stepmother) had wanted to bring me up as her own child.

My natural mother had had TB and been told not to have a baby. But somebody passed a remark to Daddy about not being able to produce a child and my mother felt guilty and responsible for these jibes and for Daddy's pain. So they must have decided then to have a baby. When I was born I was taken immediately from my mother – which must have been very hard for her as well as for me.

When I broke down as an adult the memory of the sexual relationship wasn't the major problem. The image I had was of being trapped in a playpen trying to get at my mother – that was the big image. And no matter how hard I tried I couldn't get my mother's attention – so therefore I mustn't be loveable – there must be something wrong with me. I think that was the basic problem really.

In this image of the playpen – my mother was on the other side of the room and there were people, other adults, around her, but I wasn't allowed near her. I just knew she was my mother but you see the doctors had told her that she couldn't hold me or she would give me the TB. Well, all I wanted was to be in her arms as a baby. So anything less than that was no good. There were plenty of women around who did look after me, but they weren't any good to me, they weren't what I wanted. I know these other women held me, but I also know that they wouldn't have sufficed.

I remember once having an image of desperately trying to get out of her womb so I wouldn't be blamed for her death. I would say that was one of the big factors in my becoming a religious. The idea of pregnancy and the horror of pregnancy was to me the fear of death. Even before I became aware of that, the idea of pregnancy frightened me, but I didn't know where it came from.

I was about a year old when my mother died. I would say that my father blamed himself for my mother's death and at some point he must have found me a terrible burden. I then felt responsible for all Daddy's pain as well as for my mother's death.

My father used to drink a lot and I remember as a teenager him saying that he didn't know whether he was an alcoholic or a heavy drinker. We'd laugh it off. But he was always gentle. He became kind of maudlin rather than aggressive when he was drunk.

He remarried when I was four. We'd lived with friends in between. Daddy needed somebody to look after me. I don't remember the wedding, I don't think I was there, but I remember staying with cousins and seeing Mammy (my stepmother) coming in and being told by the cousins that she was my mother.

I felt that I had been important to Daddy and all of a sudden there was somebody else there (my new mother). Then a year after they were married my brother was born. We'd moved house and I suppose it was generally a very confusing time for me. Nothing was explained. When my brother arrived I resented him because I had been the centre of whatever there was. I'm not sure if I'd been the centre of anything – but certainly he ousted me from anything that had been there. I had felt I was important to Daddy and all of a sudden there was somebody else there.

Daddy was very quiet but Mammy had an amazing respect for him. She wouldn't have had an independent thought and whatever Daddy said went. I had much more respect for Daddy's thinking than I had for Mammy's at the time.

From the time I heard of Maria Goretti I began

bargaining with God. I became very holy as a teenager and very sad. I carried this whole weight of guilt and became very good in a sad sort of way. My memory of my teen years was that I used to play the piano. The piano was my companion.

I wouldn't have had many friends. It's not that people wouldn't have liked me – they would have seen me as too good. I think I was also trying to placate adults, people of my own age weren't very significant. I think I was afraid of people of my own age getting to know me in case they'd find out about me and judge me. I was equally afraid of the adults but felt if I played my cards right, they'd think I was okay. Looking back now I'd say I tried to placate adults because they were the mother figure – I was placating mother. I think that was also a factor in going into religious life – I was looking for mother.

When I finally found out about my mother's death, when I was about eleven, there was no connection made between my birth and her death. But years later it was associated with my birth. An aunt passed a remark that my birth had killed my mother. Which isn't to say that I was to blame, but there it was anyway.

About nine years ago I was on retreat. I was very depressed and suicidal at the time. I remember doing an "active imagination" meditation. I got this image of a Victorian woman who was looking after a baby. I described her quite distinctly. I didn't know whether the baby was me or my mother. I felt I was in some sort of way in communication with my mother and my grandmother. They asked forgiveness of me for the burden of the guilt that I had carried – that they had never intended it.

She speaks in a whisper, her voice barely audible.

Then I made enquiries about my grandmother and saw her photograph. I discovered that my image was exactly as she had looked although I had no recollection of her. She had died when I was very young. She had cancer and when my mother died she just gave up. So in some way I had felt responsible for both of their deaths.

I had a full blown breakdown when I came back from Africa and ended up going to the psychiatrist. I hadn't fully realised that he was a psychiatrist when I went to him. If I had known he was I probably wouldn't have gone because the idea of me "all-together Michaela" going to a psychiatrist was a very big change of image. He was a very nice fatherly figure – very kind, and I worked with him for a year. We talked about the sexual relationship with the boy and about my mother and my fears. I was afraid of my own shadow and of everybody else and what people would think. It was very obvious to all and sundry that I wasn't coping. For ages I really was so envious of people whom I knew who were going through a bad patch but nobody knew about it. But everybody knew about *me*. Later that became a great freedom, I didn't have to keep up the mask any longer. For a long time I was afraid of what was going on inside me and terrified of other people's judgements.

That summer I went to the Holy Land and I lost my faith there. Seeing three religions fighting over a little patch of ground had an awful effect on me. I said "surely God can't mean that." So whatever shred of faith I had before, that was now gone. I hit into a terrible depression and despair and I reckoned that I really had to do something drastic. I went to a residential therapy place. I found much of that experience extremely difficult. I was very frightened, again I was afraid of judgement. I felt so mixed up and feared that the therapists, who seemed to be so together, would be judging me. I was angry with myself for messing up my life.

I think the fact that I had appeared so together in the past, and that all my affirmation had come from being together, meant that it was a major disaster that I was in such a mess. This was probably more so for me than for a lot of other people who had a realisation that they didn't have to be perfect. It was very frightening, but it was also very healing.

I was a long time in therapy, talking about the sexual relationship, before the horror of abuse hit me. Nobody had ever suggested that I had been abused. I had talked about this relationship with the boy, and then one day awful feelings of the helplessness came. I put those feelings of helplessness down to this relationship and yet the depth of the feelings that I had and the memories didn't really add up. I wasn't able to figure it out. All I knew was that I was very upset.

I talked about the abuse with this boy for about three years before I was really able to get into the feelings. Before that I had been talking about abuse up in my head really. I had gone to a therapist with a view to looking at the whole thing of abuse. I knew it was really bothering me and knew I wasn't able to deal with it. I still kept putting off dealing with it.

I remember the day I began talking about it. I talked about it as if it was somebody else that I saw out there – that it really wasn't me. The first time the abuse happened with the boy was on Christmas night. We were playing hide-and-seek and he followed me. I was under a bed and he got under the bed and he began feeling me. I remember being taken aback even as a child, but not feeling that I could say that he couldn't or shouldn't do it. He began coming to the house and again he started feeling me and encouraging me to masturbate him. I was never really sure whether I liked it or not. I was very ambivalent about it but I certainly wasn't feeling guilty about it.

Last year I had this image of being squashed. An image of a beach ball being squashed and then I had this awful feeling of being under a man and being raped and being very, very small. I remembered a penis being put into my mouth. I had often wondered about oral sex because I remember being at the dentist and the dentist trying to take X-rays. I always gagged terribly. He never managed to take the X-rays and I always felt there was something not quite normal about it because I was getting too anxious. Yet I had no memory of anything until recently.

Then one day I got this image of me wanting to be with Daddy and going in to him in his bed. I had a very vivid memory of what the house was like, although I hadn't been in it for years. I also had a very clear image of his room and the room I was in with somebody else who was looking after me. I went back to the house recently and asked if I could see it. It was exactly as I had remembered it in this image. I don't know whether he was drunk. Many people would say that it must have been some sort of fabricated memory – you can't just remember things like that. If you've forgotten them for years how can you remember that far back? I know it's a body memory and it makes so much more sense. It explains why I wasn't frightened of what the boy did to me, yet my feelings were upsetting me even though I was unable to remember what had been so distressing.

When the memory of my father abusing me surfaced I was horrified. It was the most awful shock.

We pause for a few minutes. She resumes, speaking very slowly.

It took me a while to deal with it in therapy and I was very angry with him. He had been dead for many years before I had this memory. When he died I was shocked. I had thought I'd be absolutely broken because he was all I had and I thought he was wonderful. Then when he died I wasn't as broken as I thought I'd be.

The year after his death was hard. I suppose in many ways I realised that although I loved him we really had never communicated. It's as if there was a kind of a glass wall between us. He never said how he felt and I never said how I felt. What I really wanted to ask him about was my mother but I didn't want to upset him, so therefore I didn't ask him. He never talked about my mother. I was taking responsibility for his feelings.

In many ways we were very alike. We'd talk about music. I suppose we were both into mega denial really. He would have been a romantic and an idealist in many ways and life just hadn't worked out for him. My memory of him was that he never judged anybody – but

I'd say he was blaming himself which is much like I was as well. I'd never have judged anybody else but I'd have been very hard on myself.

When he died, he died suddenly. I had had two dreams that he had died, in the fortnight before his death – which helped. So when I was told he was very ill I knew he was dead. I think the biggest shock was that he wasn't buried with my mother. That hadn't crossed my mind. Seemingly if somebody marries a second time they're buried with the second wife, it's understandable too in a way but it had never occurred to me. I found that hard. I never really wanted to visit the grave.

I never told Mammy about Daddy abusing me although I did tell her I had been abused. I was very upset at the time because I was right in the middle of dealing with my abuse. She asked me if it was Daddy and I said "no, it wasn't." At that time I had only remembered the boy abusing me. It's not something that has come up since, and she's as well off not knowing. There's no benefit in informing her now that I was also abused by Daddy. The abuse would have happened before they were married, probably before they had even met. I think the abuse with my father only happened once.

Looking back now I realise that it took me a long time to deal with my feelings. I went into orbit for a while. Then when I started to deal with my feelings I was very angry with Daddy. Before that I went through a stage when I developed a problem with a male God. I realised that I was afraid of Him. I was afraid of this big dangerous God and needed a female God. But since I acknowledged to myself that it was Daddy who had abused me and realised how that affected my idea of a male God I ceased to be afraid of Him. It didn't matter whether he was male or female.

I went through all sorts of feelings of anger towards Daddy, like wanting to cut up his penis.

She stops for a long time. She clutches a tissue in her hands and stares into space.

But now I can feel compassion for him. I think that it was very hard for him to have lost his wife. Very hard to have had a little child. In those days people didn't know what effect these things had on kids. I'm quite sure at times he resented me being around and being saddled with me. It was bad enough for him not to have his wife, but I complicated his life a lot for him.

In a funny sort of a way I don't think I need to forgive him. I don't think there's anything to forgive. I don't think he deliberately meant to hurt me. I think he may have been drunk or he may not have been. He was a very confused man. I know it has had a lasting effect on me. It was something that shouldn't have happened, but at this point, somehow I can't say that he was to blame. He just seemed to have been a very mixed-up man with sexual needs. I had my needs, I just wanted to be with him. I wanted to be loved by him. I think people were so confused about sex anyway back then.

Can I forgive him? To forgive someone seems to acknowledge that this person has done something wrong or bad that you have to forgive. I have been badly hurt, there is no doubt at all about that. But I now see my father as a little helpless child, I don't see him as an adult. I don't think he was an adult, I think he was a child in an adult's body. He never got any chances in life. He went into a job he didn't like. He always had financial pressures. Then he lost his wife. He was a very intelligent and deep-thinking man. He just didn't get a chance. He didn't grow. He was busy fitting in with what other people wanted. He was very like me. I just see him as being as helpless as I was. So there's nothing to forgive. There is a letting go of a need to forgive.

Her voice is choked with tears.

I realise that it was only in the 1980s that people began to talk about abuse or know anything about it. I think children were probably fair game a lot of the time. I think that men just presumed that they could get their sexual needs met wherever they could. I see him as probably being very sexually frustrated. I just know how mixed up and upset I was at all of my feelings, including the sexual feelings that I had repressed. Because of the whole legacy of abuse I had no desire to be in a sexual relationship.

The abuse took away my childhood. I would say for a long time it took away my sense of being a woman, because I didn't want to be feminine, I didn't want to be attractive. I wanted to be pleasing to these women figures but I certainly didn't want to be attractive to men. The idea of marriage is not attractive to me. I would find it very difficult to have a sexual relationship with a man.

I didn't have an ordinary childhood, just playing games and being a child. But I think maybe my mother's death did that anyway. I set about looking after Daddy from a very early age. When he got married again I felt I was pushed to the sidelines.

I find it very hard to differentiate between the effect my mother's death had on me and the effect the abuse had on me. I know from research that when a child is abused it is generally within the context of other trauma. I think it can be hard to differentiate. That kind of child is already vulnerable.

I lost a sense of my identity, a sense of who I was. I now have a sense of who I am, but it has been after a long haul. It was very hard to show who I was and because I was hiding it from other people I was also hiding it from myself. I used to be a good singer and actor but I stopped singing because people used to say my voice was beautiful, but I felt my inside was terrible. I felt if people saw who I was they would condemn me or reject me or judge me. So it has been very central to how I developed as a human being and how I became a workaholic – just running away from all of that pain.

In a way I was performing all my life. I used to be sorry for people who were feeling and suffering. I thought I was so lucky not to have feelings – they complicated life. I enjoyed acting and I knew I was good at it. I enjoyed singing and I knew I was good at that too. My whole life was a performance, including the smile that I had on my face all of the time. I was this happy person who needed approval extremely badly. I thought I was wonderful and other people did too. I had no sense of something being missing inside.

The effort of keeping this up twenty-four hours a day was a huge strain. I didn't realise how much of a strain it was until somebody told me about how often I talked about gritting my teeth and keeping going. I didn't hear myself saying that. When the breakdown came it was so big that I wasn't able to keep going. It did me a big favour and I'm very grateful for that.

I was very angry for a long while because I felt I had entered religious life for the wrong reasons. Once I became aware of all that happened to me I asked myself why I had entered and what was I doing here. I thought I had entered because I had this big call from God, this yearning. I did have a yearning but it was to be accepted as I was. A yearning for myself in a way.

I thought things would change when I broke down, I expected them to because I wasn't the way I had been . . .

Her tears spill over again.

But the sisters have been so good and I have got the most amazing support. I think very few people would have been encouraged to have as much therapy as I have had and to really find myself. They supported me financially and emotionally when I needed it and I'm grateful for that.

Now instead of being angry for having entered the convent for the wrong reasons I have a real sense of companionship with women. We have a terrific respect for each others' journey and for our own journey. That's really important. I've also learned to be at home with my own body. I want to be at home with all aspects of myself so that I can become whole.

Entering the convent removed the burden of sexuality from me. I felt that I was avoiding marriage by entering. I never stood up for myself in any relationship, even though I seemed very assertive. I could stand up for everything else except for my own personal needs. If I felt injustice was being done to children in school I fought for them, but I never felt I had a right to fight for myself. If anything went wrong I felt it was my own fault.

I often compare myself now to a tree with very deep roots. It's a very big strong tree and I realise that roots spread underground for a long time before they can be seen. I realise that a lot of the growing that has been going on in me in the last ten years or so I haven't been able to see. Every so often I get a glimpse of how far I've come. A few years ago I would have felt that I was really grateful to be allowed to be alive – God hadn't killed me stone dead. I had killed my mother, I had had a sexual relationship – all reasons for being killed. So I felt grateful to be allowed to live, and that was part of the bargaining with God that I wouldn't have been aware of. I'm grateful that I've been able to stick at it and that I'm worth it. Life is very good for me now. In fact it's wonderful.

I am aware of pain and sadness, but life is very good. I have a sense of who I am. My friends know my story, I don't have to apologise for it. A lot of people in my religious community know it as well and I don't have to apologise there either. I've been accepted, and that's been important. I'm able to be myself, state my needs and know that I have a right to get them met. I think that I've gone through a lot of my life believing that I would never get my needs met. I also feel much closer to my family and able to be myself with them. I love my stepmother and feel close to all my family.

I don't see people as a threat to me any more. There are vulnerable people, confused people, happy people – whatever they are I can let them be. I used to be very threatened by high-pitched women's voices. I've traced that back to around the time that my mother was probably dying or dead. Her sisters were all shouting and fighting about what was going to happen to me. I was probably somewhere around and heard all these voices and my name being mentioned, so I thought I must have been to blame for something. So whenever I heard high-pitched voices I would say "oh my God, it must be something that I've done." I used to think that when somebody was in a bad mood it was my fault. Now I don't get hooked into other people's agendas. That's very freeing and very liberating. I can let other people be and I don't allow myself to be manipulated by them.

For the future I want to be true to myself. I don't want to do things because other people think I should be doing them. I want to do things because it comes out of my heart or my need and it's what's right for me.

I feel much more at home in religious life now than I have done for a few years. I had thought seriously of leaving because I thought I had entered for the wrong reasons. I thought I was different from everybody else. But now I realise there are lots of people on the same journey as I am, with the same questions.

Now I relate to a sense of the God within. I don't practise religion in the conventional sense now any more. My community respect that. I see myself now as a woman who is searching and for whom spirituality is extremely important. I've a great sense of things coming together I've very good female friends and I've a very good male friend who's been really good for me and I've been good for him. He understands. He knows my journey and he understands where I'm coming from. He accepts me exactly as I am and that's very important and healing for me. My relationship with this male friend has enabled me to grow in trust in a male/female friendship in a way that respects my boundaries. I feel very blessed in this friendship. Now I feel at ease with men – men have their own struggle.

I don't know what the future will bring but I think I will stay within the religious community. The companionship of my own age group of women is very important. In a way I feel I've the best of worlds. I've no desire to be married, I'm very clear about that. I love children but I've no desire to have a child of my own. I've been so busy looking after "little Michaela" all my life that I never wanted a child. I also link it back to my mother as well – the idea that birth is not life giving.

So often concentrating on what another person has done to you can distract you from what is going on inside yourself. Daddy is dead, I've let go of him. I hope he is resting in peace with my mother and I believe he is. I believe that both of them believe that they have burdened me and they feel as helpless about that as I felt helpless.

She can only speak slowly and with difficulty.

I want them to rest in peace and be removed from the burden of what they have put on me. I can deal with my pain and I have the support I need to do so. I believe they won't rest in peace until I'm at peace, and I'm getting there.

We're never fully sorted out – it's a life time's journey and I want to continue on this journey.

HELP NUMBERS

NB: IF YOU ARE NOT SATISFIED WITH THE COUNSELLING HELP YOU RECEIVE TRY ALTERNATIVE COUNSELLORS UNTIL YOU FIND THE RIGHT PERSON FOR YOU.

If you have been sexually abused as a child and would like to talk to somebody the following list of contact numbers may be useful.

RAPE CRISIS CENTRES

There are a number of Rape Crisis Centres around the country who offer a professional counselling service to those who have been sexually abused.

BELFAST
Belfast Rape Crisis Centre   0801 232 249 696

CORK
Cork Rape Crisis Centre   1 800 496 496 (Freephone)
26 McCurtain Street   021 505577
Cork

DONEGAL
Rape Crisis Centre   1 800 448 844 (Freephone)
Port Road   074 28211
Co Donegal

DUBLIN
Dublin Rape Crisis Centre   1 800 778888 (Freephone)
70 Lower Leeson Street   01 661 4911
Dublin 2

GALWAY
Galway Rape Crisis Centre   1 800 355355 (Freephone)
3 St Augustine Street   091 564 983
Galway City
Galway

KERRY
Tralee Rape Crisis Centre   1 800 633333 (Freephone)
11 Denny Street   066 29588 or 23122
Tralee
Co Kerry

KILKENNY
Kilkenny Rape Crisis Centre   1 800 478478 (Freephone)
5 Dean Street   056 51555
Kilkenny

LIMERICK
Limerick Rape Crisis Centre   1 800 311511 (Freephone)
11 Upper Mallow Street   061 311 511
Limerick City
Limerick

MAYO
Mayo Rape Crisis Centre   1 800 234900 (Freephone)
Elephant Street   094 25657
Castlebar
Co Mayo

OFFALY
Tullamore Rape Crisis Centre   1 800 323232 (Freephone)
                               0506 22500

SOUTH LEINSTER
South Leinster Rape Crisis Centre 1 800 727 737 (Freephone)
Waterford Road   0503 33807
Kilkenny

TIPPERARY
Clonmel Rape Crisis Centre   1 800 340 340 (Freephone)
20 Mary Street   052 27677 / 27676
Clonmel
Co Tipperary

WATERFORD
Waterford Rape Crisis Centre   1 800 296 296 (Freephone)
2a Waterside   051 873362

WESTMEATH
Athlone Rape Crisis Centre   1 800 306 600 (Freephone)
4 Roselevin Court   0902 73815
Athlone
Co Westmeath

WEXFORD
Wexford Rape Crisis Centre   053 22722

There is also a group in BELFAST called NEXUS who provide a counselling service for adult survivors of sexual abuse. Tel: 080 1232 326803

EASTERN HEALTH BOARD (Dublin, Kildare, Wicklow)

The Eastern Health Board has established a special counselling service for the adult survivors of sexual abuse – LARAGH COUNSELLING SERVICE in Clontarf. Tel: 01 833 5044. Laragh Counselling Service is staffed by psychologists and counsellors and it operates an open referral system i.e. people can make direct contact with this service themselves.

MIDLAND HEALTH BOARD (Laois, Longford, Offaly, Westmeath)

The following is a list of contacts where the adult survivors of sexual abuse can seek help.

1. Senior Clinical Psychologist (Adult Psychiatric Services), Longford/Westmeath, St Loman's Hospital, Mullingar. Tel: 044 40191.

2. Clinical Psychologist (Adult Psychiatric Services), Community Mental Health Services, Mullingar. Tel: 044 45078 (Direct Line) 044 40221.

3. Acting Senior Clinical Psychologist/Psychiatrist, Adult Psychiatric Services, Laois/Offaly, St Fintan's Hospital, Portlaoise. Tel: 0502 21205.

4. Senior Clinical Psychologist, Longford/Westmeath Community Care, Health Centre, Dublin Road, Longford. Tel: 043 46211.

5. Child and Family Support Centres – Tullamore 0506 22488 Portlaoise 0502 62300.

There is no charge for these services.

The Midland Health Board also suggests that if a person wants to attend a private psychologist they can contact the Psychological Society of Ireland, 13 Adelaide Road, Dublin 2. Tel: 01 478 3916. The Psychological Society will give them a list of psychologists in their local area.

MID WESTERN HEALTH BOARD (Limerick, Clare, Tipperary North Riding)

The Mid Western Health Board has a number of psychologists who can be contacted directly for help and advice.

1. Noreen Harrington, Willowdale Day Hospital, Raheen, Limerick. Tel: 061 302 248.

2. Brian O'Keeffe, Tevere Day Hospital, Shelbourne Road, Limerick. Tel: 061 452 971.

3. Simon Wale, Newcastle West Day Hospital, Churchtown, Newcastle West, Limerick. Tel: 069 61799.

4. Deirdre O'Donnell / Michael Reen, Our Lady's Hospital, Ennis. Tel: 065 21414.

5. Edel O'Hara, St Mary's Health Centre, Parnell Street, Thurles. Tel: 0504 23211.

6. Eamon Butler, Glenroyd, Tyone, Nenagh. Tel: 067 33866.

7. Eddie O'Dea, Psychologist, St Anne's Day Hospital, Roxborough Road, Limerick. Tel: 061 315177.

NORTH EASTERN HEALTH BOARD (Cavan, Louth, Meath, Monaghan)

The following numbers can be contacted directly for information.

LOUTH/MEATH AREA
>   The Duty Doctor/Consultant
>   St Brigid's Hospital, Ardee
>   Tel: 041 53264

>   Dr Bernadette O'Keeffe
>   Director of Community Care
>   Tel: 042 32287

CAVAN/MONAGHAN
>   The Family Therapy Unit
>   St Davnet's Hospital, Monaghan
>   Tel: 047 81822

>   Dr Imelda Lynskey
>   Director of Community Care
>   Cavan Tel: 049 61822

NAVAN
>Dr Peter Finnegan,
>Director of Community Care
>Tel: 046 21595

DROGHEDA
>Regional Child and Family Centre
>Tel: 041 30990

If you wish to have a list of GPs in your own area please contact the GP unit at 046 27275.

NORTH WESTERN HEALTH BOARD (Donegal, Leitrim, Sligo)

There are a range of services available from the Health Board for the adult survivors of sexual abuse.

1. Psychological support including individual and group therapy services. For Donegal area contact 074 31391 or 074 22322. For Sligo/Leitrim area contact 071 55100.

2. Mental Health services including treatment and counselling. Donegal area 074 21022 or 074 22322. Sligo/Leitrim area 071 55100.

3. Social Work Support Service. Donegal area 074 31391 or 074 22322. Sligo/Leitrim area 071 55100.

Services are also provided by the following agencies:

Sligo Social Service Council
Group counselling provided. Contact Nuala Doherty
Tel: 071 45682

Boyle Family Centre
Counselling and workshops provided
Tel: 079 63000

Support is also provided by the
Women's Centre, Letterkenny
Tel: 074 24985

Women's Refuge Centre
Tel: 074 26267

SOUTH EASTERN HEALTH BOARD (Carlow, Kilkenny, Tipperary, Waterford, Wexford)

Under the Psychiatric Services Programme, Clinical Psychologists are employed in a counselling role. However for someone to use these services, they must be referred to the Psychiatric Service, which may not be appropriate or acceptable for many people. At a local level the Board's four Social Work Departments act as a first point of contact for people in difficulties.

1. Wexford Community Care Social Work Department
Tel: 053 47718
(No Adult Psychology Service)

2. Waterford Community Care Social Work Department
Tel: 051 77847

St Patrick's Hospital, John's Hill, Waterford
Tel: 051 876111

3. Waterford Adult Psychology Service
Tel: 051 74991

4. Kilkenny Community Care Social Work Department
Patrick Street, Kilkenny
Tel: 056 52208

5. Kilkenny Adult Psychology Service
Tel: 056 52341

6. Carlow Community Care Social Work Department
Athy Road, Carlow
Tel: 0503 30053

7. Carlow Adult Psychology Services
Tel: 0503 31106

8. South Tipperary Community Care Social Work Department
Western Road, Clonmel, Co Tipperary
Tel: 052 22011

9. South Tipperary Adult Psychology Service
Tel: 052 21900

SOUTHERN HEALTH BOARD (Cork, Kerry)

The following is a list of contact numbers of people who are interested in and available to counsel the adult survivors of sexual abuse.

1. Dr Breda McLeavey, Clinical Psychologist
Cork University Hospital
Tel: 021 546400

2. Prof Robert Daly, Clinical Director
Cork University Hospital
Tel: 021 546400

3. Colm Downing, Clinical Psychologist
Tralee General Hospital
Tel: 066 26222

4. Anne Culloty, Social Worker
Tralee General Hospital
Tel: 066 26222

The above services are in addition to the facilities the Health Board provides through funding the Cork and Kerry Rape Crisis Centres.

WESTERN HEALTH BOARD (Galway, Mayo, Roscommon)

The following are a list of contact numbers that adult survivors of sexual abuse may contact.

1. Director of Community Care
Community Care Offices
25 Newcastle Road Galway Tel: 091 523122

2. Director of Community Care,
Community Care Office
Western Health Board
Roscommon Tel: 0903 26518

3. Director of Community Care
Community Care Office
County Clinic
Castlebar Co Mayo Tel: 094 22333

THERE ARE MANY PRIVATE COUNSELLORS AND THERAPISTS THROUGHOUT IRELAND. YOUR NEAREST RAPE CRISIS CENTRE SHOULD BE ABLE TO PROVIDE YOU WITH A LIST OF SUITABLE PEOPLE.

IF YOU ARE LOOKING FOR HELP ELSEWHERE PLEASE CHECK THAT YOUR PROSPECTIVE COUNSELLOR/THERAPIST HAS HAD EXPERIENCE IN THE FIELD OF CHILD SEXUAL ABUSE AND HOLDS A RECOGNISED QUALIFICATION.

SOME HELP NUMBERS IN THE UK

LONDON RAPE AND SEXUAL ABUSE SUPPORT CENTRE
Open Monday to Friday 12.00pm – 3.30pm and 7.00pm – 9.30pm.
Saturday, Sunday and Bank Holidays 2.30pm – 5.00pm.
Tel: 00 44 181 1122 (if phoning from Ireland).
0181 239 1122 (in the UK).

LONDON WOMEN'S AID
Open 10.00pm – 4.30pm (closed 1.00 – 2.00).
Tel: 00 44 171 392 2092 (if phoning from Ireland).
0171 392 2092 (in the UK).

LONDON IRISH WOMEN'S CENTRE
The centre will provide information regarding therapists/counsellors in the UK.
Tel: 00 44 171 249 7318 (if phoning from Ireland).
0171 249 7318 (in the UK).

LONDON RAPE CRISIS CENTRE
Open Monday to Friday 6.00pm – 10.00pm.
Saturday and Sunday 10.00am – 10.00pm.
(Callers phoning may be given the number of a counsellor on duty.)
Tel: 00 44 171 837 1600 (if phoning from Ireland).
0171 837 1600 (in the UK).

USEFUL BOOKS

The following books were found useful by some of the survivors who spoke to me. This is not intended to be a comprehensive list.

The Courage to Heal by Ellen Bass and Laura Davis. Published by Cedar.

What About Me? by Grant Cameron. Published by Eden Grove Edition.

Surviving Sexual Abuse by Rosemary Liddy and Deirdre Walsh. Published by Attic Press.

NOTES

NOTES

NOTES

NOTES

NOTES